The Missionary Manual

A Handbook Of Methods For Missionary Work In Young People's Societies

By

Amos R. Wells

First Fruits Press
Wilmore, Kentucky
c2015

The missionary manual: a handbook of methods for missionary work in young people's societies, by Amos R. Wells.

First Fruits Press, ©2015
Previously published: Boston and Chicago: United Society of Christian Endeavor, ©1899.

ISBN: 9781621713951 (print), 9781621713968 (digital)

Digital version at http://place.asburyseminary.edu/christianendeavorbooks/21/

Wells, Amos R. (Amos Russel), 1862-1933.
    The missionary manual : a handbook of methods for missionary work in young people's societies / by Amos R. Wells.
    134 pages ; 21 cm.
    Wilmore, Ky. : First Fruits Press, ©2015.
    Reprint. Previously published: Boston : United Society of Christian Endeavor, ©1899.
    ISBN: 9781621713951 (pbk.)
    1. International Society of Christian Endeavor. 2. Missions I. Title.
BV2095 .W4 2015

Cover design by Jonathan Ramsay

asburyseminary.edu
800.2ASBURY
204 North Lexington Avenue
Wilmore, Kentucky 40390

First Fruits
THE ACADEMIC OPEN PRESS OF ASBURY SEMINARY

First Fruits Press
The Academic Open Press of Asbury Theological Seminary
204 N. Lexington Ave., Wilmore, KY 40390
859-858-2236
first.fruits@asburyseminary.edu
asbury.to/firstfruits

THE
MISSIONARY MANUAL

A HANDBOOK OF METHODS FOR MISSIONARY WORK IN YOUNG PEOPLE'S SOCIETIES

BY

AMOS R. WELLS

AUTHOR OF " PRAYER-MEETING METHODS," " THE JUNIOR MANUAL," ETC.

BOSTON AND CHICAGO
UNITED SOCIETY OF CHRISTIAN ENDEAVOR

Plimpton Press

Printers and Binders, Norwood, Mass.

U. S. A.

PREFACE.

No set of workers in our young people's societies is so eager for work to do, or so enthusiastic in doing the work, as our missionary committees. These energetic laborers have long needed a full and systematic manual of directions and suggestions, such as this book aims to be. A few volumes have taken up this task in part and with admirable success, but none with the completeness of detail or anything like the fullness that I have attempted.

Those that use this book will find it practical. Indeed, at least half of the plans here set forth have been tried and proved by large numbers of societies all over the world.

At the same time, however, recognizing the value of novelty in this work as in most work, I have made up the volume to a very large extent — probably half — of original plans which have not before been published. I trust that these new methods will be found as useful as the old have been, and that they will give fresh life to thousands of missionary meetings.

The book has been written with the one purpose of promoting the growth of the Kingdom of God. May our Saviour use it to that end.

AMOS R. WELLS.

Boston, June, 1899.

CONTENTS.

THE MISSIONARY MANUAL.

CHAPTER I.

A MISSIONARY SOCIETY.

IT was a Great Dismal Swamp.

The ground was oozy underneath, and the matted trees shut out the sky from above. Through the tangled thickets crept poisonous things, and the only paths were beaten down by savage beasts. Foul birds of prey found the woods full of carcasses. The air was heavy with miasmas, and a terrible silence was everywhere, except when it was broken by a scream that was worse than silence.

Men lived in this swamp — men and women and little children. Though one can hardly say they lived, so dreadful were their lives in their wretched hovels, surrounded with the terror of the jungle, and cruel with all the wildness of the tigers and the cobras.

In this swamp there was born, one happy day, a little babe who grew up to be a carpenter. That was what the people called him — the Carpenter — though he did work that no carpenter ever did before. For not only did he build noble homes in place of the filthy huts, but he taught the people how to make drains so that the ground became sweet and firm. How to quarry rock to lay upon this firm ground.

7

How to cut roads through the jungle and let in the blessed sunlight and the clean, purifying air. How to build a city with splendid public edifices and merry, peaceful homes. How to raise the lofty cathedral in the midst of it all.

And then the Carpenter died; but as he died, almost with his last breath he said to the weeping men around him: "Do not stop here. Go ye into all the swamp and redeem it. Go ye. Go."

Then for a few years they obeyed the Carpenter's behest, and extended the borders of their pleasant city wonderfully. But before long they began to grow lazy, and quite too well satisfied with the fair domain already won. They built a high wall over which no tiger could leap. They soon forgot that there was a swamp beyond, and the Carpenter's last words passed entirely out of memory.

But the miasma was there, and often it crept over the wall and stole in swift desolation among the marble palaces. And the tigers were there, nor could these selfish folks quite close their ears to the screams of the tigers' victims. For still there were millions of people in the swamp, and still it extended for leagues beyond the city of the Carpenter — an ever-present threat and a silent accusation.

*   *   *

The story is a sad one, because it is true. God be praised that with every year it is growing less true! God be praised that he gives us young people some share in the draining of the swamp, in obeying the blessed Carpenter!

This is to be the motive of our missionary work — simple obedience. "Go ye," Christ has said; "make disciples of all nations." And it is our life to obey.

No other incentive is needed to make every Christian Endeavor society a missionary society. There is no need of the addition of our impelling motto, "For Christ and the Church." There is no need to urge that missionary work will increase the members' interest in the society, that it will brighten all the prayer meetings, stimulate the singing, vivify the testimony, make the prayers vital; that it will send us all with new zest to the Bible; that it will inculcate a liking for the best reading, make us more liberal in every direction, and greatly improve the discipline of the society by setting all its members to work; that it widens immensely the intelligence, putting us in touch with the most important of events, with the most essential history. All of this is true, and all of it adds to the argument for making our societies missionary societies. But it is all on too low a level for those that have taken our great pledge to do "whatever He would like to have us do."

Thy command is enough, Lord Jesus. Thy words are the way of joy, and we will follow therein. Thy kingdom come, and Thy will be done, on earth as it is in heaven. For Thine is the kingdom, and the power, and the glory.

CHAPTER II.

THE MISSIONARY COMMITTEE.

What It Is. — If any committee in the society should consist of enthusiasts, it is this committee. If any should be inventive and persistent, courageous and prayerful, it is these workers for the advancement of the Kingdom. They should not be mere theorists. No one can hope to get others interested in missions who is not a missionary himself; who is not ready, that is, to go anywhere God wants him to go, and do whatever God wants him to do, to win souls for Christ, — and this although he may go no farther than his own household, or the family next door.

The committee should be a praying committee. It will fail if it does not remember its power: "Lo, I am with you alway."

No one should be placed upon this committee for the sake of converting him to missions; let the committee do that. It may be necessary to place upon this committee a few of the workers for term after term; but if they are genuine missionary enthusiasts, the society will gain thereby. Only — let the committee never forget that its success, and its only success, lies in making the other Endeavorers as enthusiastic as the committeemen are themselves.

Definite Aims. — The mission field is so extensive that no committee has greater need of definite aims than the missionary committee. Choose these goals early in the term of office. Be specific: so many books to be read by each member; so much money to be given; so many missionary meetings to be held; so much information to be presented and mastered. Do not be too ambitious, or you will accomplish nothing; but anything is better than not being ambitious enough!

In Every Meeting. — Seek to get into every regular prayer meeting of the society something about missions. Nearly every topic presented to our Christian Endeavor societies has its missionary aspect. Appoint different members of the committee in turn to develop this side of the theme.

The Committee Organized. — Subdivide the work of the committee so that each may know what he has to do, and be responsible for some particular task. One may be the secretary; another the treasurer, and have charge, not only of the collecting of money, but of the Tenth Legion, and of other spurs to increased benevolence. Another may be librarian, unless it seems best to give the library in charge of some Endeavorer outside the committee. At any rate, he will seek to promote missionary reading and study. Still another will be corresponding secretary, and carry on the letter-writing. The relief work will be placed in the hands of another, the missionary meetings in the hands of another, the missionary socials will be assigned to another, the work in newspaper and magazine clipping to another, and so on. Each committeeman will be chairman of the entire committee for the purpose of carrying on his especial work; and each month, for the sake of variety and drill, these tasks will be shifted.

The Nucleus. — It may not be possible at once to organize a missionary study class in your society, outside of the missionary committee; but that committee itself should surely constitute itself a study class, and go right ahead in the systematic pursuit of missionary information. It should meet regularly and often — say once every two weeks; and each committee meeting should be a meeting for the study of some missionary field, or other definite missionary theme. If a five-minute report of each of these studies is given to the society at its next meeting, and if the report is brightly made, it will not be long before the other Endeavorers will begin to question whether such study would not be a good thing for them also.

Committee Leadership. — For training and for variety, let the entire committee lead the first missionary meeting of the season. The committee will sit facing the society, and some part in the work of leading will be assigned to each by the chairman. Thus the society will learn, at the very outset of the term, just who are on the missionary committee, and the members of the committee will be impressed with their responsibility.

Home and Foreign Committees. — For some reason — chiefly the abundance of good literature on the foreign fields — most missionary meetings, of young folks and old folks alike, deal with the foreign rather than the home fields, and this in spite of the fact that the preference of most Christian pocketbooks is for the home-mission collection-box. Now, of course, we believe that the field is one, at home or abroad, and to make sure of an even presentation of its needs it may be well to divide the missionary committee into two sub-committees, one for home and the other for foreign missions, each to conduct a meeting in turn. Let the various members of the committee take turns in serving on each of these committees.

Personal Work. — Divide the members of the society among the committeemen, giving each a group of Endeavorers with whom he may talk, to get them interested in missions. One may need to read more; another, perhaps, ought to be giving more; a third should be influenced to pray more for missions, and so on.

A Scrap-Book Apiece. — Some societies have a pleasant system of assigning to each member of the missionary committee a missionary country upon which he collects all kinds of clippings, pictures, and the like, and pastes them in a scrap-book given him for that purpose. Of course the committeemen exchange scraps and aid one another. At the close of the term of office these scrap-books are presented to the society, each being prefaced with a written message from its editor, and the whole forms a fine addition to the missionary library. As an adjunct to this labor, the several committeemen may be asked to correspond each of them with a missionary in the country he is studying for his scrap-book.

CHAPTER III.

MISSIONARY MEETINGS.

A Good Missionary Meeting should be different from the last good missionary meeting. It should present missionary information not only in such a way that it can be remembered, but in such a way that it cannot be forgotten. It should not only make missionary students, but create mission-lovers. If your meeting puts people to sleep, it matters not how good it is— or, rather, it is not good at all. There is not in all the world a subject more interesting than missions, and uninteresting missionary meetings are the most inexcusable kind of uninteresting meetings. That the missionary meeting should be spiritual, that it should be full of the spirit of prayer, that it should instruct, that it should promote beneficence—all this, although it may sound strange to say it—comes after the one requirement that it be interesting. Interest in missions once gained, the marvellous facts will do the rest; they will provoke prayers and gifts and earnest study.

With these beliefs in mind, I have planned and collected the following schemes for missionary meetings. They will certainly be found to be diversified, and I know they are workable. It is my prayer that they may be *worked!*

Be Original.—The plans given in this chapter—

and, for that matter, in this entire book — are not to take the place of your own invention. They are intended to help you form your own plans and to supplement the plans you may form yourself. Indeed, your own plan is better for you than a much better plan that is not your own, and your society, as well as yourself, is likely to take more interest in it. Use printed exercises, but also make up your own; and use these schemes for missionary meetings, but also get up a few on your own account.

Missionary Bands. — This is an ideal plan for missionary work, provided it is not held to so long that it becomes stereotyped. Divide the society into as many groups as your denomination has important mission fields — the China Band, the Japan Band, the African Band, etc. Each band will have a leader who will superintend its work. It will be the business of the bands to study their respective countries and prepare meetings upon them to be held during the year, each band presiding over its own meeting. Thus you are quite sure that every member of the society will do some definite missionary reading, and also that all the missionary work of your denomination will be laid before the society during the year. A beneficial emulation among the bands is likely to be aroused, each striving to present the best meeting.

The Number of Missionary Meetings to be held during the year depends, of course, on the progress already made in missionary interest. Four are laid down in the uniform topics prepared by the United Society of Christian Endeavor, one each quarter; but as soon as the society has developed sufficient enthusiasm to warrant it, by all means drop some of the other topics and substitute missionary meetings for them. You should have at least as many missionary meetings in the course of the year as your denomination has important mission fields.

The Topics of the regular missionary meetings laid down in the United Society's list of topics are of necessity general. The societies may substitute for these general topics the consideration of special fields in which they are interested, or they may use the general topic and add to it whatever exercises they please bearing on their special studies. If the general topic is used, it is well for the missionary committee to prepare a large number of practical questions applying that topic to the actual missionary work of their denomination. Give these questions to the members beforehand, that they may come prepared to answer them in the meeting.

When It Is Timely. — The missionary committee should be prompt to seize upon subjects of timely interest. While the war was in progress between this country and Spain was the time of all others in which to arouse interest in missions in Spain and the West Indies. Do not hesitate to break in upon your programme whenever any missionary country comes into special prominence, and hold a meeting upon that country.

The Meeting Before the missionary meeting should always be made a preparation for it, to a certain extent. The plans for that meeting should be unfolded, unless even longer notice has been necessary. Whatever is required from the members should be clearly explained, and prayers should be offered for its success.

Keep the Pledge. — Missionary meetings are very likely to be filled up with a few speakers. This should be avoided as often as possible, but whenever it seems best that only a few should take part at length, be sure to give some opportunity in the course of the meeting for every one to fulfil his pledge to "take some part in every meeting." Sentence prayers for missions afford one opportunity; the repeating of missionary Bible verses, another. In calling for this, expressly request those to whom parts have been assigned for the evening not to take part in this exercise. An excellent way is at the close of the meeting to ask the entire society to rise and as their participation in the meeting to read in concert some appropriate hymn from the song-book, or some passage from the Bible that has been copied on a large sheet of paper or on the blackboard, so that all can read it.

Assignment Slips. — Do not trust to folks' memories. Whenever the missionary committee wants anything done by a member — whether it be to write an essay, make a talk, lead in prayer, or read a single item — let it write upon a piece of paper the member's name, date of the meeting, subject, and time alloted. Then there will be no mistake about it.

Appropriate Decorations should not be reserved for the missionary social alone. Use them to brighten up the regular missionary meeting also. The flag of the country you are to study, a vase full of the flowers associated with it, pictures of mission scenes on the walls, even though they are not referred to during the evening, have their effect and contribute to the interest.

Do Not Read. — Many missionary meetings are quite spoiled by the dull reading of selections from periodicals. This is the cheapest, easiest, and least effective method of carrying on a missionary meeting. Better present a single fact, looking your audience in the eye and using your own natural words, than present fifty facts in the most eloquent language, if the language is another's, and you have to read it. "Say it in your own words" should be the constant exhortation of the missionary committee whenever they give out missionary articles or books upon which a report is expected.

The Last Ten Minutes of a regular meeting may be set aside for a course of missionary study if you cannot get systematic missionary information before the society in any other way. This weekly ten minutes, if wisely used, filled with pointed essays and bright talks, the whole being fixed by short questions, will soon suffice to give the Endeavorers an outline of missionary history in general and the history of your denomination's missions in particular.

An Examination may well be held at the close of each missionary meeting. Announce at the opening of the meeting that it will be held. Appoint one of the best members to conduct it. Give him five minutes for the exercise. He will ask sharp, pointed questions, which can be answered in few words, and which cover the important points of information brought out during the evening. The answers are to be given in concert, and if they are weak on any point, the examiner will ask the same question over again further on.

A Summarist. — If for any reason it is not thought best to hold the examination, appoint a "summarist," who will watch the evening's exercises carefully and fill a few minutes at the end with a review of the most important points brought out. Be sure to save time for him. The danger of our missionary meetings is that they will leave nothing behind them in the mind. Nothing is taught unless something is remembered. Remember that!

Home Missions. — The difficulty of getting good material for home-mission meetings should make you especially zealous for this branch of the subject. Try to hold as many home-mission meetings as foreign. Spend one evening telling the noble story of how Whitman saved Oregon. Spend another on Brainerd and Eliot and the other early missionaries to the Indians. Such a book as Puddefoot's "Minutemen on the Frontier" (New York: T. Y. Crowell and Co. $1.25) or any of Egerton R. Young's books, will prove of intense interest. Subscribe to all the home-mission magazines you can. You will find them pulsing with the life-blood of heroes.

Use the Student Volunteers, if any are in your neighborhood. These earnest young men and women are always glad to address young people's societies on the subject so dear to their hearts, and a meeting led by one of them serves a double purpose — it inspires and instructs the society, and it shows the volunteers that we are deeply interested in their work and purposes.

Anniversaries. — Make a list of the days of birth or of death of great missionaries, and hold meetings occasionally, on or near such anniversaries, to consider their lives. For example, John E. Clough was born on June 16, and Fidelia Fiske arrived at Oroomiah on June 14, and Carey sailed for India, and Judson reached Burmah, on June 13 — anniversaries that should add much interest to any missionary meeting held during that week. "The Missionary Daily Text-Book" (New York: The Fleming H. Revell Co.) is a useful compilation, if any one is in search of these facts.

"The Missionary Bulletin." — This is a home-made missionary periodical. It may appear once a quarter or oftener. Its editor should be some one interested in missions, and also — a good coaxer! He will write the editorials, and as little besides as he can. Fill the paper with thoughts upon missions, original poems, bits of mission news collected by the members, spurs to more generous giving. Do not forget a bit of fun now and then. Put it in regular newspaper form, and do not omit the advertisements. Even these, however, should be harmonious, for you may advertise for missionary pocketbooks, missionary hands, and missionary tongues.

"Fuel for Missionary Fires" is a book by Belle M. Brain, published by the United Society of Christian Endeavor, and sold for 35 cents. It furnishes a great deal of material for missionary meetings, and is supplementary to the present volume, treating with great fulness a number of valuable plans for mission-ary meetings, and supplying a fund of misssionary quotations and the like. All missionary committees should have it.

Missionary Exercises that deal with the work of all denominations are not easy to find, and so I mention here the series published by the United Society of Christian Endeavor. This series is especially full in the subjects connected with the American continent.

A Biography Meeting. — One of the best kinds of missionary meetings is based simply on a single heroic life devoted to the great cause. Get as many copies of the biography as you can, and set as many as possible to reading it. If you have only one copy, those that are to participate in the meeting might well gather in some home and read the book together, each taking notes on the part he is to talk about. Divide the life by topics. If Carey, for instance, is the theme, you will ask one to tell about his antecedents and early life; another to tell about the beginning of the first missionary society; others to describe the establishment of the first English mission, the Serampore Brotherhood, Carey's work as a translator, as a teacher, as a practical business man, as a scientist, as a preacher, a soul-winner, the story of his death, the summary of his life work. Maps and all sorts of pictures showing Hindoo places and customs should be exhibited. If each person speaks briefly and to the point, such a meeting as this, dealing with such men as Martyn, Paton, Mackay, Patteson, Duff, Heber, Morrison, Gilmour, Hannington, Moffatt, Livingstone, Judson, Hamlin, Coan, and others almost beyond number, cannot fail to leave behind it a profound impression, and to influence for missions all that are present, and especially those that take part.

A Progress Meeting. — This meeting might come at the end of the year's work. It is for the purpose of noting the encouraging omens all over the world. Assign the different mission fields to different Endeavorers, and instruct each to note the favorable signs in the region he is treating. If there are dark clouds, for this once pass them by. Make it a hallelujah meeting.

A Catechism Meeting. — One of the most attractive of missionary meetings, a meeting especially valuable because of the number of Endeavorers it brings in, is one made up entirely of questions and answers. The leader or the committee must prepare beforehand as many questions as there are members in the society, and write out short answers for the more inexperienced, or give them the facts that they may write out answers for themselves. Here is a sample set of such questions : —

How many Christians are in the world, and how many not Christians?

How much would an average yearly gift of one dollar from each Protestant in the world increase the funds of the foreign-mission boards?

How much per member does our denomination give each year for home missions? for foreign missions?

In what country are our denominational missions now most flourishing? least flourishing?

Is there any country or group of islands in the world to which the gospel of Christ has not been taken?

What is the most discouraging mission field?

Whom do you consider the three greatest missionaries to Africa?

What missions of our denomination are the oldest?

What country has the most missions of our denomination?

What mission field of our denomination has been completely won, and the work closed up?

In what parts of India are our denominational missions?

What is the greatest missionary society in the world?

In what country do Methodist missions lead all others? Congregational?

When was our foreign missionary society formed?

Who were the first missionaries of our denomination?

Where, at present, are the leading centres of our own home-mission work?

What missionary periodicals does our church publish?

Who do you think are the six greatest men among our denominational missionaries of the past and present?

In general, what is the present condition of our missions in Japan?

How much money has this society pledged to missions for this year?

What is tithe-giving, and what are its advantages?

What is the most interesting book on missions you ever read?

Who is your favorite missionary hero?

What are some of the words of Christ that command missionary enterprises?

It will be seen that these questions are intended to arouse original thought, as well as to promote investigation and give a sort of bird's-eye view of the mission field. Scores of such questions can be answered in the course of an hour. It is a good plan to save time at the close of the meeting for a review, the same questions being asked at random, and the entire society being expected to reply in concert. Or at another meeting the programme may be repeated without change for the purpose of fixing the facts in mind.

A Language Meeting.— So much of missionary success has been based upon the study of the strange languages of this Babel of a world that a missionary meeting may with profit be based upon the same

study. Take, for instance, a large home-made outline
map of India. Make from brightly colored adhesive
paper a set of circular wafers, one color for each of
India's great dialects — the Hindi, Marathi, Telugu,
Tamil, etc. Each wafer will be given to a different
Endeavorer, who will come forward when the leader
calls and fix it to the map in the proper place, at the
same time telling something about the language —
how many persons speak it, what great missionaries
have worked in that region, something about the character of the people, and the like. In this way the
polyglot nation of Egypt may be studied, and even
such a country as China, whose languages are not so
diverse — yet here there are the languages of the different classes, the written and the spoken languages.
The difficulties of these different tongues, the triumphs
missionaries have won over them, the pioneers in
language-study in each country, the influence of translations and of the establishment of a native literature
— all these and many similar themes will readily come
to mind. Of course, if you can, you will get hold of
the foreigners themselves, and get audible specimens
of the languages you are studying.

Missionary Women.— Since so large a part of the
Endeavorers are young women, we should have at
least one meeting entirely devoted to missionary
heroines. Buckland's "Women in the Mission Field"
(New York: Thomas Whittaker. 50 cents) will furnish abundant material, but it should be supplemented
with studies of the women that are now doing noble
work for your own missionary boards, and with such
famous stories as that of Mrs. Judson.

A Modern Miracles Meeting.— The wonderful happenings on the mission field are the nearest approach to miracles we have in modern times, and furnish the most convincing proofs of Christianity. Using such books as Dr. Pierson's " Miracles of Missions," first and second series (New York: Funk and Wagnalls, $1.00) crowd some evening full of brief accounts of these marvellous events. When you tell about the " Lone Star " mission, hang a silver star before the audience. When you tell about Murray's work for the blind in China, hang by the side of the star a pair of dark glasses. A small spear, the point dipped in red ink, or a rainbow of pasteboard nicely painted, will illustrate the story of Madagascar. In the same way other symbols may be added as the evening progresses.

Medical Missions will make a splendid theme for a separate meeting. The story of Dr. Mackenzie, in Beach's " Knights of the Labarum," (Chicago: Student Volunteer Movement) is a sample of the many inspiring lives that may be studied. The missionary magazines are full of noble proofs of the value of medical missions, and short anecdotes may be collected to almost any extent. The meeting might well begin with a recital of the need in heathen countries of care for the body. It is a gruesome tale. Several Endeavorers should speak, each taking up one country. Then should come the stories of medical missions, and of how they have opened the way for the gospel. Close with the song, " The Great Physician."

A Curio Meeting.— To this meeting each member will bring some object from missionary lands, if only a picture of a foreign scene. He will exhibit this to the society and say a word about missions in line with what he has shown. Do not announce this meeting until by private interviews you have assured yourself of a basis for its success.

A Picture Meeting.— This is so much like the curio meeting that it should not be held the same year. Ask every member of the society to bring some missionary picture, and tell something about it. It may be a scene in China, the picture of a Parsee priest, the portrait of a missionary, a sketch of a South African kraal, a scrap of Chinese printing. Whatever it is, let it be shown and a word be said about it. The society should sit in a compact body that the pictures may readily be seen, and at the close they might be passed from hand to hand, the title being written upon each. In this way much may be learned, and very pleasantly.

Missionary Debates.— Two or more will speak on a side, according to the time you have at your disposal. Of course there will be no display of oratory, only an earnest presentation of the case from the differing view-points. "Was Henry Martyn's life a failure or a success?" is a possible subject, although a rather one-sided one. Other suggestions are these: "Is it advisable to send out unmarried missionaries?" "Should our missionaries engage to any considerable extent in the work of secular education?" "Is it best that missionaries should labor in secular occupations for the support of their missions?"

A Board Meeting.— If your denomination has several missionary boards, hold one meeting early in the year, in which you will try to fix clearly the different lines of activity of the various boards. Divide the evening among them, and treat each in a succession of talks or little essays, whose subjects might be: the history of the board, its present field of work, its great men, the books and magazines connected with its work, its present needs, its most glorious triumphs.

A One-Field Meeting.—It is often well to spend an entire evening upon one particular field. I do not mean a single country but a portion of a country, such as the province of Foochow, the Tamil district of South India, the Dakota tribe of Indians. The minute knowledge that can thus be gained gives one a sense of mastery such as a wider survey cannot give.

A Missionary Picnic.—The essence of a picnic is that everybody brings something. Get up a missionary meeting on that plan, having it understood that each person in the society is to bring some item of missionary interest. The leader will place before the society a map of the world, and will point to each mission field as he calls for the items from that field that may have been brought. After each field, call for brief prayers for the work there, especially remembering the needs of the persons that may have been mentioned in the items contributed. The missionary committee should have a few items ready to give out to the careless, but if the plan is thoroughly announced for several weeks beforehand, these items will hardly be drawn upon.

A Twelve-Facts Meeting.—At the rate of one fact a minute, you can get into the hour five times twelve facts, with the probability that time enough will be left for the opening, for singing, and for prayers. Choose, therefore, five important 'missionary fields, such as China, India, Africa, South America, and the home field. Take sixty Endeavorers, and ask each to come prepared to give one missionary fact belonging to the country assigned him. If you have fewer than sixty members, appoint some to double duty. Let all the facts about China, say, be given first. Follow with prayers for China, then go on to the other countries.

Denominational Dates. — To fix the times when the various missionary boards of your denomination were founded, and when they began work in various fields, as well as the dates of other events important in the missionary history of your denomination, make a series of pasteboard squares, and in each print one of these dates, with a brief statement of the fact, as: "Home Board founded, 1836." Give each placard to an Endeavorer, with instructions to say a few words on that subject. Set in front of the room a wooden upright. Hooks in this correspond to eyes in the placards, which are hung upon the upright, as the talks are made, in the order of the years, thus forming a kind of denominational family tree.

A Map Meeting. — Issue a call for short missionary items, to be written out in the language of the member and read by him at the meeting. Each Endeavorer will go to the front of the room, read his item, and then pin it upon a map of the world in the proper place. Of course it will be better if you have a series of large home-made maps of the various mission countries, as these will not be injured by the pins and will show the geography on a larger scale than a map of the world.

An Impersonation Meeting. — Ask a number of members to study up, each of them, the life of some living missionary in such a way that he can speak in that missionary's character at the coming meeting. Representing Dr. Greene, for instance, John Saunders will tell something about his own work among the Coreans, using the first person all the way through. The meeting may be varied by assigning to some members such characters as a native Persian, an Arab, a Mohammedan priest, a Jew of Russia. Have your brightest speaker lead off in this exercise, to set the pace for the rest.

A Diagram Meeting. — Give each member a missionary fact that can be illustrated by a diagram, and get him to prepare it and show it at the next missionary meeting, with an explanation. Such a book as " The Missionary Pastor " (New York : Fleming H. Revell Co. 75 cents) will be very helpful here. For example, the gifts to foreign missions by decades in the present century may be shown by a number of squares, each gloriously larger than the one before it. Islam may be shown as a tree, and on the branches may be written the names of some of the dreadful things that are the outgrowths from that false faith.

A Missionary Tour through different missionary lands will make up a good meeting. Appoint a separate guide for each stage of the journey.

Suppose you desire to go to Siam. One Endeavorer will take you across our country, not forgetting to point out the great home-mission fields. A second guide will put you on board ship at San Francisco and carry you to Hawaii, escorting you around those islands and telling you of their wonderful missionary history. So by easy stages you will get to Japan, to Shanghai, to the Malay Peninsula, and finally complete your journey with a tour of Siam. Limit each guide to five minutes.

Heroes and Heroines. — For this meeting ask each member to name some missionary that has done great things for God, telling one of the great things accomplished. Of course the country in which the missionary works should be named, and some member of the society should sit by a map with a pointer to locate each missionary as he is named. It will add interest to the meeting if the young women be asked to name missionary heroines and the young men missionary heroes!

A Kingdom-Come Meeting. — Ask each member in preparation for this meeting to think over the history of the past month and choose some event that has a definite relation to the coming of the Kingdom. Then let him tell what that relation is. It may be immediate, such as the granting of freer religious liberty in a South American state, or it may be less direct, such as an improvement in printing.

Around the Christian Endeavor World. — An evening spent in a review of Christian Endeavor in all lands may be made full of missionary interest. It will show us the possibilities of the natives as few other exhibits can. A file of *The Christian Endeavor World* will furnish an abundance of material in the way of reports and pictures. A little exertion will obtain for you a letter from some native Endeavorer in each mission field of the world.

A Missionary Question-Box. — You will not go far in your missionary studies without exciting questions, and an opportunity for these should be given. The first question-box need occupy only part of an evening, and the missionary committee should provide a number of questions to be used in case the members of the society are not in an interrogative mood. Questions may be expected on the different religions, on different plans of missionary organization, on problems of tithe-giving, on the customs of the heathen world, on the progress of the Kingdom. The leader should invite to the meeting some of the best informed church-members, to whom he may refer the more difficult questions.

An Answer-Box is similar, except that a general question is propounded and the society is asked to contribute answers to it. Some such questions as these may be used for answer-boxes: "What is the chief qualification for missionary work?" "What is the most interesting story of missions?" "Who was the world's greatest missionary? Why?" "Why should we give at least a tenth of our incomes to the Lord?"

A Missionary News-Box is made up of bits of missionary information contributed by all the members. Every one must put in something, and no one may put in more than three items. Limit the total number of words to one hundred, so that, if any one gives two or three items, each must be very short indeed. After the items have been collected, redistribute them and have them read, no one reading his own.

A Prophecy Meeting. — One speaker will tell the worst things he knows about heathen lands, picturing the darkness of the dark countries under their degrading religions. He will be followed by other speakers who will prophesy of the future that Christianity will inaugurate. One will tell what changes may be expected as a result of the entrance of Christian commerce and civilization. Another will foresee the coming triumphs of Christian education. Others will speak of what God is going to accomplish through Christian commerce, Christian literature, Christian physicians. Others will tell of coming changes in society and government, in the homes and the daily life.

A One-Missionary Evening. — This is to introduce some living missionary in whom the society may come to have a personal interest — not a great missionary, perhaps, but one who has visited the church or is related to some church-member, or some one to whom you have recently sent money. Find out about his early life, his college days, his missionary work. Sing his favorite hymns. Get letters from him, and have them read. Show his photograph. Pray for him and for his converts.

" Early in the Morning." — There is much in the interest aroused by novel surroundings, and a meeting held at a time different from usual is almost certain to be better than usual. Some societies have applied this principle to missionary meetings, and have found that a missionary meeting held the very first thing on the Lord's Day gives a magnificent start to the day, and stirs up fresh zeal for missions.   There is a special fitness in it, too, since missions mean the sunrise of hope and joy for the nations.

Missionary Camps. — Divide the society into groups, which you will call camps — the Indian camp, the African camp, the Japanese camp, etc.   They will sit together, the chairs being arranged in circles, and each camp will have five minutes in which to fire off guns at the rest.   The " guns " consist of missionary items about the country from which their camp takes its name.

A Quotation Meeting. — Choose three missionaries that are good writers — for example, Gilmour of Mongolia, Patteson of the South Seas, and Martyn of India and Persia.   Make extracts from their writings and give them to a number of Endeavorers to read, asking each to comment briefly on the sentiment expressed.   Follow each set of quotations with a short talk on the life of the missionary.

Missionary Martyrs. — This topic is a thrilling one for a missionary meeting.   To make it a success you will need a pretty wide knowledge of missionary biography, or some such book as Croil's " The Noble Army of Martyrs " (Philadelphia: The Presbyterian Board of Publication. 75 cents).   Assign to different members the stories of these heroic deaths, and close the evening with a talk by the pastor on the lessons they teach.

Bible Translation. — The story of the translation of the Bible into the hundreds of languages which, before the advent of the missionary, were not even written languages, is one of the finest stories of human history, and well deserves an evening to itself. Different members may undertake to give accounts of the history of Bible translation in different countries, and each speaker will become an enthusiast on his theme. In addition, great heroism has been displayed by the Bible colporters of the world, and wonderful results have sprung from their labors. The American Bible Society has a leaflet for free distribution giving samples of the various languages into which the Bible has been translated.

A Patience Meeting. — Patience is a lesson all missionaries and missionary workers have to learn, and the rewards of patience have been illustrated on almost every mission field. It will pay you to gather up, some evening, the stories of the world's prominent mission fields that have had a tedious, tiresome beginning, years dragging on without a single convert, and then a sunburst of success. Nearly every missionary biography and the history of nearly every mission field will afford you material for this meeting.

A Missionary Trial is thus conducted. Appoint a judge and a jury, and two lawyers for each of the three divisions of the debate. The question is, "Which agency is doing most for India,— medical missions, missionary literature, or evangelism?" One from each side will speak first, and then the second set of speakers. The judge will charge the jury, and finally a verdict will be brought in.

A Home Meeting will be a pleasant novelty. The entire society will be invited to a missionary meeting in some private house. The informal arrangement of the chairs, the piano for the music, the novel surroundings, the atlas and globe and other resources of the library at hand, the possibility of passing pictures around among the company — all combine to make a meeting that will be remembered.

An Exploration Meeting. — This is an imaginary journey to a missionary land made by a party of Christian explorers, who will report in the first person, as if each had actually seen what he describes. There will be a geographer, who will describe the physical condition of the country, its size, and the like. Then will come the statistician, who will tell about the population, and give other figures, as if he had compiled them himself. Next will come the historian, who will tell what he has learned from the people about their national history. The rambler will come next, and will describe some of the queer customs he has observed. Two press reporters will speak, one of them giving some conversations he has held with the people about their systems of government and of education and the social conditions generally, and the other describing his observations on missionary work in the country. Of course the geographer has made a map and the rest of them had their cameras and took snapshots, which will furnish the pictures for the evening. Some of these travellers, too, may have brought back curios from the journey.

A Missionary Congress. — This meeting may be greatly varied. Here is one form of it: Three persons are chosen to represent each important missionary country, and at the meeting each of the three is presented to the society in order. First will come a native priest, who will tell about the heathen religion of the land. Next will come a native woman, who will describe the condition of women under the rule of heathenism. Finally will come a Christian convert, who will tell about missions and what they have done for his country. These characters may well be dressed in the native costume, if it can be obtained.

A Missionary Newspaper Evening. — Current events in their bearing on missions make a fascinating theme for study; since the missionary now as always is in the forefront of civilization, and where its battles are the hottest, he is always to be found. The war between India and China was closely involved with missionary interests. So were the massacres in Armenia. So was the war in Cuba, that in Matabeleland, that of the French in Madagascar, and, indeed, almost every considerable event of recent years has had its important missionary aspects. Besides this, the newspapers are full of smaller details that have a bearing on missions — the coming of large numbers of Japanese to Hawaii, the purchase of the Caroline Islands by Germany, the building of a new railroad in China, the election of a Mormon to Congress, trouble in an Indian tribe. To make this meeting a success, give each Endeavorer a particular paper to watch, and this will give him a feeling of responsibility, even though several are set to report upon the same paper. It will also be necessary to give help to the inexperienced, whose missionary eyes are hardly yet opened.

The Bible and Missions. — Select for each member of the society some Bible verse bearing on missions, asking him to read it in the next meeting and tell just *how* it bears on missions. If you are sure the society will do it, it will be better to permit them to choose their own Bible verses.

A Statistics Meeting may seem like a formidable undertaking, but if you once try it, you will find it a meeting full of unexpected felicities. Use all kinds of statistics bearing on missions, and leave it largely to the persons to whom you give the figures to present them in attractive ways. Be sure, however, to suggest these ways to persons that may not think of them themselves. The rapidly increasing number of Christians in the world, for instance, has been illustrated by the figure of a man standing in water which is rising as Christianity grows. During the first century it comes up to his ankles, and with each following period it rises over a greater space.

A Bird's-Eye View of missionary history is a meeting easy to prepare and very instructive, needing only some such book as Bliss's "Concise History of Missions" (New York: Fleming H. Revell Co. 75 cents.) or Leonard's "Hundred Years of Missions" (New York: Funk and Wagnalls. $1.50.) It will be a surprise to most persons to learn that modern missions did not begin with Carey. Draw on a large sheet of paper a number of vertical lines to represent the missionary history of the different countries. Draw horizontal lines across these, dividing them up into decades, or quarter centuries, as you please. Prepare pasteboard placards which are to be hung on the large diagram in the proper place. For instance, a bit of pasteboard reading "Martyn, 1811," hung in the proper place on the line marked "Persia," will show the beginning of missions in that empire, and it should be put in place with a word about that saintly young man, his visit to Persia, and his translation of the New Testament into the language of the country. When you are done, you will have a summary which you will be glad to keep standing before the society in future missionary meetings.

Native Heroism. — Divide this inspiring subject among the committees, asking the prayer-meeting committee, for instance, to bring to the meeting examples of the heroism of African converts, the lookout committee to do the same for Japan, etc. Almost any missionary biography or history will furnish you with many examples. So, also, will current missionary literature.

"The Ten Greatest Missionaries" may furnish the basis of a missionary programme. The missionary committee will wish to select them, and I will not even give my own list,— which is as well, since you would not agree to it! Each of the ten lives may be considered, in different aspects, by more than one Endeavorer. Do not try to be exhaustive. For Livingstone, for instance, it will be enough if one speaks of his personal character, a second of his prominent missionary achievements, a third of the circumstances attending his death.

Your Own Denomination — who are its greatest missionaries? This will be a good question to discuss at some missionary meeting. Make sure that the claims of all the most prominent missionaries are brought forward during the evening, and thus you will get a review of denominational mission fields. Use a map, and place on the scene of each missionary's labors a gilt star bearing the initial of his name.

An Other-Denominations Meeting.— One of the great gains from our Christian Endeavor interdenominational movement is this, that it is showing each one of us how much of noble endeavor and Christlike zeal is in other denominations besides our own. Even the largest and most missionary of denominations is doing only a fraction of the world's missionary work, and we are making a great mistake if in our missionary meetings, as is so often done, we narrow our vision to our own denominational fields. The Presbyterians, for instance, have Siam practically to themselves; the Congregationalists have Turkey; the United Presbyterians have Egypt, and so on. But do not all denominations need to know how the kingdom of God is progressing in Siam, Turkey, Egypt, and the rest? Besides, very likely our own denomination is not doing the largest or the most successful work in India or China or Japan. Do we not want to know what that work is, and to get the inspiration it will give? Of course to prepare this " other denominations " meeting requires much study, but if you have the " Encyclopedia of Missions," it will not be difficult. Use a map of the world. Make adhesive labels to stick on the countries where each denomination is at work — blue for the Presbyterians, red for the Methodists, etc. It will not be possible to tell in every case, but wherever in any country one denomination has clear precedence over the others, add a gilt star to its label. Facts of interest about the missionary work of the other denominations will be presented as these labels are placed on the map.

Note. — The books mentioned in this chapter, and throughout the book, may all be obtained, if desired, at the prices quoted, from the United Society of Christian Endeavor, Tremont Temple, Boston.

CHAPTER IV.

MISSIONARY MAPS.

The Use of Maps. — Missionary meetings without maps are meetings hung in the air. They do not leave any definite impression. On the other hand, when maps and similar devices make the attack on Eye-gate, the citadel of attention and memory is soon ours. Do not take it for granted that any place in foreign lands, however familiar to you, is familiar to your auditors; and however often you have already pointed it out, point it out again whenever you come across it in the meeting, for the sake of the new members and for the forgetful among the old members.

Home-Made Maps are the essentials; "boughten" maps are the luxuries. The home-made maps are the best because the process of making them has taught somebody something, and because, since they are mere outlines, one may insert just what is needed for the subject under discussion, and leave the rest out. Moreover, with the home-made map you can make free use of those prime aids to the missionary worker, the colored gummed "stickers." Do not be over-critical in drawing these maps. It is not necessary to get in every bay and every curve of every river. Make a few measurements and locate carefully the principal features of the map, filling in the rest of the outline with eye measurements only.

A Map-Drawing Evening might be held by the mis-

sionary committee at the beginning of its year's work.
Draft whatever assistance you think you will need.
Provide a dozen sheets or more of heavy manilla
paper, ink, coarse pens, black crayon, and water-color
paints. If you have not a good letterer in your number, use stencils or cut out letters from a printer's
alphabet. Then set to work and turn out the year's
supply of home-made outline maps.

Hectographed Maps are an improvement even over
the maps I have been describing, because every member of the society can have one, and can take it home
as a souvenir of the meeting and for further study and
review. Besides, these maps can be made very simple, and the Endeavorers can be set to putting in
various features as they are described during the
evening. This work of theirs will serve to impress
the facts upon them.

The Published Maps of mission fields, however, are
of great value for reference, and you should get them
by all means, if you can, and keep them in view of
the society at all its meetings. A large missionary
map of the world may be obtained from the Student
Volunteer Movement, 283 Fourth Ave., New York
City, for $3.00. Several of the missionary boards
publish maps of their principal mission fields.

Charts of All Kinds may be manufactured by our en-
terprising committee. A circle may be divided into
radiating sections, each of a size proportioned to the
numbers in some great religion of the world. When
these sections are colored so as to be readily distin-
guished, the chart will furnish a striking argument for
missions. The "spheres of influence" of the Eu-

ropean nations in Africa and in China may be shown by the use of colors on outline maps. Gilt stars may show where your society has sent contributions this year. Red hearts, each bearing the initial of a missionary, may indicate where the chief missionaries of your denomination are at work. You may illustrate the fact that China has one medical missionary to two and one half million people, and the United States four thousand physicians to the same population, by making two squares of the same size, placing in the centre of one a single dot, and filling the other with four thousand dots. You may make a set of squares proportioned in size to the population of the different countries. In short, there is no end to the bright ways in which consecrated pencils, managed by consecrated brains, can preach in black and white.

Relief Maps showing the principal facts about the country's contour, the chief mountain ranges and plateaus and valleys, may easily be made, and, once made, are a joy forever. Shred newspapers and let them soak over night, when they may be beaten up into a pulp which you can use for your modeling. A temporary map may be made from damp sand or from clay. Color your board blue for the water and let this remain uncovered wherever the water is. Then build up your map, using wooden blocks for the cities, bits of evergreen for forest regions, and the like.

Dissected Maps may be made to teach missionary geography as well as secular. For example, to show the language areas of India, make a map of that great empire, color the language areas differently, mount the map and cut it apart, one language to a section.

The different parts may then be pinned to a board be-fore the society, one at a time, each in the right posi-tion, something being said about each language as it is added to the map.

Gradual Disclosure. — One of the brightest ways to use a missionary map is this. Before the meeting cover it with pieces of paper, each pinned separately, and so arranged that, as the different parts of the country are mentioned during the evening, the various pieces of paper can be removed one by one, until the whole map is disclosed.

The Comparative Sizes of the countries of the world should be shown whenever you place a map before the society. Put in one corner the State of Pennsyl-vania drawn in the proper proportion. One of the most effective missionary maps I ever saw showed China with the various European countries set off upon its surface. In the same way the New England States might be laid out in one of the great Western States of our Union, thus teaching a lesson in home missions.

A Globe is of help in showing the relative positions of places and their relative sizes, about which we get so confused an idea from the atlas. Little flags may flutter from the globe here and there where mission-aries of your denomination are at work.

A Blackboard is a decided help, because upon it you can dash off your map as you talk, and rub out what is no longer needed. Whatever medium you use, whether blackboard or manilla paper, it is an ad-vantage not to insert the names beforehand, but to print them as you come to them in the course of the meeting.

CHAPTER V.

MISSIONARY MUSIC.

Index the Hymn-Book. — The missionary committee will be met at the outset with a difficulty in regard to the hymn-book. It will find the number of hymns placed under the category of " Missions " entirely in-adequate for a series of meetings. But of course many hymns not indexed under this subject are just as suitable for missionary meetings. Hymns of pa-tience, of courage, of faith, of perseverance, of the presence and power of the Spirit, of the spread of the Kingdom — all these are essentially missionary hymns. The committee may well devote an hour to reviewing the entire hymn-book used by the society, marking every hymn that is suitable to a missionary meeting, and becoming familiar with those that are not well known. Then make a special index of these for ready reference.

An Impressive Opening. — Choose a missionary hymn that shall be sung at all the missionary meet-ings for the year — not some flippant song, but some grand hymn of the faith. It should be committed to memory, and at the beginning of every missionary meeting the entire company should rise and sing the hymn with fervor.

A Missionary Chant will prove still more effective for this purpose. There are numbers of psalms that would make noble introductions to your missionary meetings, and the society could easily learn to chant them. Such a psalm, too, would serve as a useful interruption to the course of a missionary meeting, exalting its tone if in any way it has fallen below the high level of the start.

Enliven the Ordinary Missionary Meeting with special music. There are many noble missionary anthems. Antiphonal songs may easily be arranged from such missionary hymns, for instance, as "Watchman, tell us of the night," which breaks up so readily into question and answer. Solos may be introduced, and any good missionary hymn may be very effective if sung in this way.

The Missionaries' Hymns. — A little pleasant research will bring out many facts connecting missionaries with our best hymns. Some of them were written by missionaries. Some of them have been prompted by stirring events in missionary history. Many of them have been used in great crises on the mission fields, or in the lives of missionary heroes. An evening of song in which the result of these studies is mingled with the singing of the hymns to which they relate would be a profitable occasion.

You Can Aid the Church Missionary Meeting greatly by forming a Christian Endeavor choir for use on such occasions. No parade need be made of the fact. The young people will only sit together in any part of the room and sing with all their might. It will tell.

A Missionary Concert. — This name is applied always to a "concert of prayer" for missions. Why not get up a missionary concert, using the word in its original sense? There are many beautiful missionary anthems and solos. Each could be prefaced with a brief speech calling attention to its lesson. There are longer pieces of missionary music suitable for such an occasion. I venture to name one by Prof. T. Martin Towne and myself, entitled "Sir Money's Crusade," published by Fillmore Brothers, Cincinnati.

Native Music will add much to such a concert, and also to any missionary meeting. You may be able to get some Turk or Chinese or other native of missionary lands to sing for you. Foreign instruments will, of course, add to the interest.

Song Services in Prisons and Hospitals are lines of effort suitable for the missionary committee to take up, if you have no special committee for this blessed work. The gospel can be sung in both these places more effectively than it can be preached. The services of song at neighborhood prayer meetings might also come within the province of the missionary committee, if you have no music committee.

An Outdoor Song Service is a piece of home missionary work well worth attempting. It may be made a beautiful prelude to the evening service, if there are grounds in front of the church that are suitable for it, and it will gather to that service many that otherwise might not come. But this outdoor song service may be held (proper permission being obtained) in any part of the city that needs evangelistic effort. The sweet hymns, lifted on the fresh young voices, will prove the best of church bells, and will draw together a crowd anywhere to hear what your pastor may have to say to them. In this outdoor work it is much better if you can sing without any book, looking straight into the eyes of the crowd.

The Music Committee should, of course, work hand in hand with the missionary committee in all this, provided you have a music committee. Indeed, much of this work would properly fall to the music committee, and is here mentioned only because so few societies dignify music by assigning it to a special set of workers.

CHAPTER VI.

MISSIONARY PRAYERS.

Missions and Prayer Go Hand in Hand. — Without a sense of the Saviour's presence, and without constant real communion with him, no genuine missionary work was ever done. You must gauge the success of your labors, missionary committees, not by the size of your audience, not by the spirit of your meetings, but by the prayers they spur the Endeavorers to make spontaneously for the mission fields and missionaries in which you have been trying to interest them. Believe with all your heart that God answers prayer. Know that the prayers of Christians — prayers and what they incite us to do — are the one thing needful for the salvation of the world; God will do everything else. Pray for definite blessings upon particular men and places. Expect results. Follow up your prayers, and recognize with gratitude God's kindness in answering them.

Prayer in the Meeting. — Encourage the use of names in praying for missions in the meetings. After some especially important piece of news, let the chairman ask some one to offer prayer for the missionary or the field that has been mentioned. Pray often in the meeting for the places where your contributions have gone. The Yale Band proposes a series of topics for missionary prayer — one for each meeting for six months. If you follow these, you will bring before God in prayer all of the great phases of missionary work and all the mission fields of the world. Silent prayer for some special missionary, or sentence prayers which take up in turn the particular needs of some great mission field, are exceedingly helpful.

A Concert of Prayer. — Name for each month some especial missionary station, and call for simultaneous prayer for that station at a fixed time every day during the month. Let the station know that you are praying for their work, all of you. Of course this station will be remembered at every meeting in many ways. Some societies place on a blackboard the name of some missionary each week for the same purpose. Do not, however, confuse the members with too many calls for prayer. The essential thing is that you *expect results*, and know that God will give them.

Individual Prayer. — Every year give each member of the society the name of some missionary whom he is to consider his very own, and whom he is to remember every day in his prayers. Of course he will find out all he can about him and his work. Of course, too, he will write and tell the missionary that he is praying for him daily, and this knowledge will be to the missionary a constant well of joy and courage. Have you ever noticed how continually missionaries in their letters are urging us to pray for them? It is their one great plea, and they are very sincere in making it.

Historic Prayers. — The annals of missions are full

of wonderful answers to prayer, and the recitation of some of these would make a magnificent missionary meeting, besides spurring the members to more zeal in praying for missions. Appoint each member to some missionary life or field and ask him to give at the meeting a single instance, taken from his subject, of the proved power of prayer.

CHAPTER VII.

MISSIONARY READING.

Hand in Hand. — Missionary inspiration and missionary information go together. The way to fill missionary treasuries is to fill missionary heads. To read Paton's life is half a missionary education! To read Mackay's life is the other half! It is simply impossible for a mind of ordinary earnestness and impressibility to peruse any one of a dozen missionary biographies that might easily be named, and not henceforth be full of missionary enthusiasm. It is one of the first duties of the missionary committees to prove the truth of this statement.

A Book Evening. — It would be well to devote an entire missionary meeting to the inspiring of interest in missionary literature. Get as many different Endeavorers as possible to tell about the missionary books they have read, and what interesting thing they found in each. Get the Sunday-school librarian to bring the missionary books from the Sunday-school library, show each, and speak briefly about it. Choose bright passages from books and magazines, and have them read. Show a complete set of sample copies of the missionary magazines in which you wish to interest the society. Close with an address by your pastor on the great books of missionary literature with which every one should be acquainted.

Missionary Libraries. — One of the very best ways of establishing and increasing missionary enthusiasm is by the establishing of missionary libraries. Nowadays books are so wonderfully cheap that such an undertaking is possible for every society in the land. Before you decide that you cannot do it, write to the United Society of Christian Endeavor and ask for their circulars describing the missionary libraries they have to sell. These are all standard works, the very best and most up-to-date, and you will be astonished to see how trifling is their cost. Such a library, if you once get a nucleus and get the Endeavorers interested in it, will grow almost without your effort. It is probably best to appoint as librarian some one outside the committee, because in this way you increase the number of those interested in the cause.

To Start a Library. — Perhaps the best way is to go boldly to the members with a subscription paper, and ask them for twenty-five-cent subscriptions, making it very plain that the subscriptions are by no means limited to that amount! You will soon have enough to buy a goodly number of books. If you ask the members to give a book apiece, many may wish to have that more individual share in the new enterprise for the Master.

A Loan Library. — People are likely to appreciate more thoroughly what they pay something for. Take advantage of this principle in your missionary work. After you have established the missionary library, charge five cents apiece for the reading of the books, and a fine of a cent a day whenever the books are kept beyond two weeks. No one will object to this charge, and thus you will soon gather enough money for additions to the library.

A One-Book Meeting. — Choose the best missionary book you can find, and get as many Endeavorers to read it as there are chapters in the book. This will take time, but do it. Assign each new reader to a different chapter of the book, telling him that at a future missionary meeting he will be expected to speak for one minute on the most interesting point of that chapter. You may be preparing at the same time for several of these meetings.

The Six-Star Band. — Enroll under this name those of your society that will promise to read six missionary books during the year. Get some one to give a talk on the delights of missionary reading, and after this talk make your appeal for members of the Six-Star Band. Let them choose their own books, but have a list to suggest to them. Urge system—the reading of one book every two months. Learn how the scheme is progressing, and report from time to time before the society, that interest may be aroused and new members added to the band. Utilize this reading in the missionary meetings.

How Long? — It is an encouragement to possible readers of a book if they can know that it will not take long to read it. The missionary committee will do well to get a book read through (by a tolerably rapid reader!) before recommending it to the society. He will time himself, and every one will be astonished to learn how short a time, after all, will suffice to read a book, compared with the amount of time we spend in reading newspapers and magazines.

Bringing It Home to Each. — If you want to do especially thorough work, let each member of the missionary committee take a group of the Endeavorers and try to persuade every member of his group to read one missionary book, or some good missionary magazine, each month. If this is impossible at first, satisfy yourself with getting him to read a single bright article. The appetite will grow with what it feeds on.

Fifteen Minutes a Day. — If the members of the society think it too much to promise to read one missionary book every two months, get them to agree to spend fifteen minutes a day in missionary reading. This will mean *more* than half a book a month, but you need not tell them so! Obtain from each person that promises this a monthly report of how the plan is working, and stir up things by presenting these reports before the society, of course without mentioning names.

Book Reviews. — Any one will read a book more carefully if he knows he is to write or speak upon it later. Therefore, whenever you get the Endeavorers to read missionary books, put them down on later — not too distant — missionary programmes for essays on those books!

"To Be Continued." — One of the most useful devices, if you would arouse interest in any missionary book, is to read bits of it here and there before the society, always reading up to some climax of interest — and stopping before you reach it! If this is brightly done, you may be sure that there will be a demand for that book as soon as it is placed in the Sunday-school or the society library.

A Loan Office. — Once a Christian Endeavor social was brightly used to stimulate interest in missionary reading. A booth was mysteriously curtained off and labelled "International News Agency and Loan Office." All were urged to call at the office, and once within the solemn purlieus, they were inveigled into borrowing missionary books and promising to read them through — promises for which they were ever afterward grateful.

Ask Them. — A wise pastor once promoted interest in missionary reading simply by asking each Endeavorer to answer in writing these three questions: What kind of missionary reading do you like? Where do you find it? Would you read more if it were brought to your notice? If the missionary committee start out with such a set of inquiries, they will set the members to thinking and will find out just where they stand in the matter of missionary reading.

For Illustration. — Each member of the missionary committee may choose a missionary book some month and read it chiefly with an eye to the prayer-meeting topics of the coming month, and in order to find in it illustrations and other material suitable for use in those meetings. Thus every meeting of the next month will be a missionary meeting.

In the Public Library. — If the public library is accessible to the society, by all means make out a list of the best missionary books contained in it, with their numbers. Have the list duplicated on a manifolder, and give a copy to every member of the society, with an urging to go through the entire set of books, instead of reading so much fiction. Be sure to put on your list only interesting books.

In the Sunday-School Library.— Probably your Sunday-school library contains some delightful missionary books. Probably, too, no one reads them. Get the superintendent's permission to say a few words before the school some Sunday about these books. Put their numbers on the blackboard, and ask the teachers to interest their scholars in them. Take them out yourselves and lend them to those that can be persuaded to read them.

Call In the Sunday-School.—You may be able to gain the help of the Sunday school toward forming a missionary library in this way. Ask each Sunday-school class to add to the Sunday-school library one missionary book a year of their own selection. Of course the missionary committee will be ready to suggest good books. In this way each class will be likely at least to read its own book, and to tell every one else how good it is!

To Read Aloud.— The art of reading aloud is passing away, now that books are so common, and family interests so diversified. Try to restore it, and at the same time quicken missionary zeal, by establishing neighborhood reading circles. Get together on Essex Street the Cadwalladers, the Ashendens, and the Stanleys, who will listen to Ruth Ashenden as she reads in her clear, sympathetic tones the beautiful story of Henry Martyn. Assemble on Lincoln Avenue the Partingtons, Huntleys, and Hales, to hear Philip Huntley read Dr. Hamlin's fascinating "Life and Times." These neighborhood reading clubs will be just the thing for the long winter evenings, and their results may be used in later missionary meetings.

The Encyclopedia. — If your society can afford it — and more societies can afford it than think they can — by all means purchase a copy of the admirable Enclyclopedia of Missions, published in two volumes by Funk and Wagnalls. It is an expensive work, costing $12 unless you can get a reduction through your pastor, but it is worth every cent it costs, being the only full and authoritative compendium of the world's missionary activities. Its maps and its thousands of interesting articles will give you material for missionary meetings for a decade.

Pass Them On. — A pleasant device is the following. Bind into a home-made booklet some good missionary articles, including a missionary story and a missionary poem or two, with a few bright paragraphs to enliven it. Write on the cover a list of eight or ten Endeavorers who will pass the pamphlet from one to another in the order named, each writing below his name some comment on the pamphlet as a whole, after he has read it, or on some particular article. Of course this plan may be carried out as extensively as the committee chooses.

A Collection of Pamphlets. — Much of the most valuable missionary literature is put in pamphlets. Doubtless your denominational boards have issued many of these pamphlets, and packed into them a large amount of most interesting material, as well as complete statements regarding your denominational missionary enterprises. Many of the pamphlets are given away; others are sold at a nominal cost. For a few dollars you can buy a little library of them, not only from your board but from all the other great missionary boards of the land. After you have them, it will add much to their life, if you bind them. Do not bind them together, but separately, and a home-made binding in heavy paper will answer every purpose. And, by the way, missionary almanacs and the yearly reports of the missionary conferences will constitute an important part of this material.

A Newspaper Committee. — Much that has a distinct bearing on missions appears nowadays in the daily papers. To gather this up, appoint two or three young men as a newspaper committee, whose duty it shall be to report at each missionary meeting whatever they have seen lately in their dailies that concerns missionary progress and opportunities. Of course each young man should have access to a different newspaper.

The Use of Clippings. — It is pleasant and easy work, this collecting of clippings from periodicals ; the problem is to make use of the clippings after they are collected ! The trouble is always twofold — the clippings are not systematically arranged, and they are not frequently reviewed, so that one has in mind his various possessions. This subject is important enough to warrant the appointment of a clipping committee, to act as assistants to the missionary committee. At any rate, the missionary committee should place it among their most urgent duties.

All kinds of religious and secular periodicals will furnish material for the collection. Here you will get an illustrated article on Cuba ; next, a bright little story of missionary heroism in Peru ; and again, an editorial giving statistics of the missionary progress

among the Syrians.   Now it will be a picture showing
the Egyptian costume,.useful, possibly, in some future
missionary meeting.   Again, it will be a newspaper
map of South Africa.   So closely are all the interests
of the world related to missions that the range of these
clippings is very wide.

For their preservation and consultation, the envelope system is the most convenient.   Get a large
number of stout manilla envelopes, large enough to
hold magazine articles and pictures without folding.
Mark each with the name of the mission field and the
country.   You may go further in your classification,
and subdivide China, for instance, into Chinese
government, Chinese customs, Chinese education, and
the like.

Then, having your clippings, *use* them.   Issue them
as you would library books, numbering each clipping
and recording the name of the borrower.   See to it
that every suitable clipping is at once used in the next
missionary meeting that touches the country to which
it relates.   After it has been used in this way, place
upon it a mark signifying that fact, so that you can
distinguish at a glance what is fresh material, and
what is.not.

Interest the entire society in this enterprise, for in
no other way can you cover a wide circle of periodicals.   You will soon find that the older church members will be glad to make use of your collection in
preparing for their own missionary meetings, and will
reciprocate the favor by the addition of valuable clippings from time to time.

A File of Periodicals. — I strongly recommend your

society to gather as complete files as possible of all the missionary periodicals of your denomination, and of as many others as you can. Very likely you will find in the church those that will be glad to give their old copies, for the sake of getting rid of them. Home-made bindings will answer, if you cannot afford professional work, and they should be bound in yearly volumes. Then they should be placed in some case convenient of access to all the workers. A card catalogue of their contents should be prepared by the committee. The preparation of this will be in itself a valuable missionary training, and will furnish occupation for many pleasant committee evenings.

One to a Periodical. — To stimulate interest in the missionary periodicals, appoint one Endeavorer a special committee on this missionary periodical, another on a second, another on a third, and so on, until you have covered all the missionary periodicals of your denomination, as well as one or two general ones. These members will be called upon at regular intervals to report interesting items from their magazines and papers. It would be well to make up at least one missionary meeting during the year almost entirely of such reports.

Subscription Agents. — Your missionary committee will do most important service in the cause of missions if they will make it their business to institute a thorough canvass of the community each year, for subscriptions to the missionary periodicals of the denomination, and to such general periodicals as *The Missionary Review of the World*. Get a full set of sample copies. You can sometimes obtain bundles

of samples for free distribution.   Learn what club
rates you can get with other periodicals which your
people may be taking.   Go into the work as earnestly
as if you were to receive a large commission or a fine
premium.   You *will* receive the best of premiums —
God's blessing for helpful service.

The Missionary Review of the World. — This chapter
would not be complete without mention of this splendid aid to all missionary workers.   Your first duty is
to see that your denominational missionary magazines
are taken liberally in the society; but in addition to
this you should have in the society at least one copy
of the magazine whose scope is the missionary activities of all denominations and nations.   A file of this
magazine from the beginning would be an inexhaus-
tible mine of missionary lore.

CHAPTER VIII.

MISSIONARY STUDY CLASSES.

Easily Possible. — A missionary study class is easily within the reach of any Christian Endeavor society. Do not start with too ambitious plans, and do not wait for large numbers. Begin with few members and with tasks that are not difficult, and confidently count on experience to increase your capacity for study and enlarge your numbers. Even though no more than two of the society are willing to undertake this work, they can form a study class by themselves, and they will be likely to get quite as much good from it as they would if the class were larger!

The Best Plan for a missionary study class I have been able to devise is the following. It has been put in operation in many classes all over the country, and all that have tried it have testified to its working qualities. The constitution is self-explanatory : —

CONSTITUTION.

ARTICLE I. — NAME.

This organization will be called the Christian Endeavor Mission Club of . . . .

NOTE. — It will be pleasant for the club to choose a chapter name. The clubs usually name themselves after some famous missionary in whose work their church has an especial interest. A Baptist club, for instance, might call itself the Carey or Judson chapter ; Methodists might organize Bishop Taylor chapters ; a Presbyterian church might have a Paton chapter ; a Congregationalist church, a Coan chapter, etc.

ARTICLE II. — PURPOSE.

The purpose of this club is to read missionary books, and to gain a general knowledge of the history of missionary work of all denominations, and a full and definite knowledge of the missionary work of our own denomination in all the world.

ARTICLE III. — WORK.

The club will follow some definite course of missionary reading and study, to be laid down by its executive committee, in consultation with the pastor.

ARTICLE IV. — ORGANIZATION.

The membership of this club shall consist of all young persons interested in missions, who expect to attend most of the meetings, and to take part as their turn comes in all the work of the club.

Note. — Many clubs may wish to drop the word " young " from the foregoing, and admit older persons as well. It is especially urged that no drones shall be admitted. It is not best to seek large numbers in order to get an audience. Two earnest workers make a better club than two hundred that come merely to listen. Begin with few, if need be, but those that are genuine workers, that know the value of a knowledge of missions, and are willing to give time as well as energy to obtain it ; those, too, that are willing to take their turn in serving in each of the offices, and doing all kinds of club work.

ARTICLE V. — MEETINGS.

This club will meet every week on . . . . . evening at . . . o'clock, at the house of one of its members.

Note. — In some communities it may be best to have one regular place of meeting. Ordinarily, the interests of good fellowship would be promoted by meeting from house to house.

ARTICLE VI. — OFFICERS.

The officers of this society shall be a president, vice-president, secretary, and treasurer, elected for one year, and performing the usual duties assigned to such officers. These four constitute the executive committee.

The club also has nine peculiar offices. To the latter offices the president will assign different persons each month. These officers are : one reader, two reporters, one statistician, one examiner, one geographer, one historian or biographer, one traveller, and one reviewer.

NOTE. — It will be especially necessary to get a president that knows the importance of keeping all the exercises to their time, beginning promptly, making things run by clock-work.

The treasurer should be good at collecting the dues, when the books are purchased by systematic collections.

The secretary should send to the members notices of all meetings.

It will be the reader's business to read before the club the portion of the biography or missionary history assigned for the meeting. He should, of course, read this over beforehand. In the rare cases where it is too long for the time, he should condense it, reading the most interesting portions, and giving a synopsis of the remainder.

The two reporters will present recent missionary news. One of them will deal with the country under discussion, and the other with the rest of the world. *Only a few notes should be presented at each meeting.*

The statistician will give any missionary statistics connected with the country studied. He will get best results if he presents only one or two facts each week, emphasizing them, and illustrating them with diagrams.

The geographer will speak of the size of the country, its population, languages, etc. The traveller will tell about the character and the habits of its people. Both the latter officers will do well to present *only one or two facts at a time,*— no more than can readily be carried in the memory.

The historian will give a brief history of the progress of missions in the country.

If the history of missions is the basis of study, the historian becomes the reader, and in his place the club should have a biographer, who presents at each meeting a condensed biography, giving the salient and interesting facts regarding some eminent missionary. Where the club is reading a biography, the biographer, of course, is the reader.

The examiner will ask questions, at the end of each session, on the points brought out in each session. The reviewer will ask questions on the most important points brought out in the preceding session. The work of the examiner and reviewer is of especial importance. If questions show that what has been heard and told is not fixed in the memory, better repeat it at another meeting than permit it to go in at one ear and out at the other.

The president, vice-president, secretary, and treasurer may, if the club is small, hold, also, any four of the nine special offices, and small clubs will find it necessary to give to several of the members more than one office.

ARTICLE VII. — PROGRAMME.

The order of exercises for a meeting of a Christian Endeavor Mission Club may be the following: —

1. Singing of a missionary hymn.
2. Business.
3. Sentence prayers for the progress of missions.
4. Bible quotations bearing on missions.
5. Questions by the reviewer.
6. Report of the geographer.

7. Reading of the missionary biography or history.
8. Report of the traveller.
9. Report of the historian or biographer.
10. Report of the statistician.
11. Report of the reporter on the country studied.
12. Report of the general reporter.
13. Questions of the examiner, and general conversation.
14. Closing prayer.
15. Closing song.

NOTE. — This programme cannot successfully be carried out in less than one hour and a half. Five minutes will be enough for all officers except the reader, and one half-hour should be devoted to the reading. If the club cannot give an hour and a half to the meetings, then reports from *four* of the special officers only should be heard at one meeting, and the remaining four should be heard at the next meeting, the reader, of course, working at each meeting.

<h3 style="text-align:center">ARTICLE VIII. — BOOKS.</h3>

NOTE. — This article must be formulated by the individual clubs, according to the plans they adopt for obtaining the books.

The treasurer should take charge of the purchase of books. He may buy them anywhere; or, if more convenient, he can always obtain them from the United States Society of Christian Endeavor as cheaply as in any bookstore in the country.

A great deal of the literature used by the clubs should, of course, be obtained from the denominational missionary boards. Each club should obtain from these boards a complete list of the books and pamphlets they have for the use of their churches. Many of these pamphlets may be obtained free.

The club should subscribe to the missionary periodicals of its own denomination, and pass these about among the members.

It is very important that the club have access, at each meeting, to a good set of maps, a gazetteer, an up-to-date dictionary, and an encyclopædia. These are cumbrous books to carry around, and for this reason only it is better for the club to meet uniformly at one place.

Each member should, of course, contribute to the general use of the club whatever books or magazines he may possess bearing on the subject under discussion.

This is a pretty thorough-going scheme, and it may be necessary to modify it, especially at the start. You may not wish to hold meetings oftener than once a fortnight. You may prefer to dispense with the services of the traveller, the historian, and their com_ rades. In other ways you may wish to simplify the plan. It is given here, with that understanding, in its most complete form. The points to be insisted on, however, are regularity in the meetings and system in the work. Definite accomplishment, although it may be slight, is quite certain to create a desire for more, while haphazard work is always unsatisfactory and dissatisfying.

The Leader of the study class may well be a permanent official, if some experienced missionary student, with tact, energy, and attractiveness, can be found willing to undertake this delightful and important work. But if no permanent leader can be found, why, Christian Endeavorers are used to carrying on their work without much help. You can take turns in the leadership, and, thus divided, neither the labor nor the responsibility will be too burdensome.

The Members of the study class should be— as will be understood—those that are not afraid of a little work, but are in earnest in this matter of missions. There will be no objection, however, to permitting the attendance of visitors who will come to listen and who may catch the contagion of zeal.

The Plan of Study may follow the divisions of countries, and may take up one mission field after another, reading such books as " The Neglected Continent " for Africa, " Chinese Characteristics " for China, " The Cross in the Land of the Trident " for India, " An American Missionary in Japan " for the Sunrise Empire, and so on. Or it may proceed along biographical lines, reading one great missionary life for each country, such as Carey's for India, Gardiner's for South America, Paton's for the South Seas, Livingstone's for Africa, Gilmour's for China, Neesima's for Japan, Whitman's for America, Hamlin's for Turkey. Or the work may be a series of studies of the missionary societies, their fields and their accomplishments. Or at times it may deal with current topics in relation to missions. General biographies are best to begin with, and then books about the countries as a whole.

The Books for the study class should be purchased by contribution from all the members. If this plan of reading aloud is pursued, one book will last for several months. The members of the class may prefer to buy the books in turn, each to keep for his own the book he has bought. Or the books may be given to the society to serve as the nucleus of a missionary library, or to the Sunday-school library. Generally speaking, short books should be chosen, and models for this purpose are the missionary biographies and many other missionary books published by the Fleming H. Revell Company, and the publications issued by the Student Volunteer Movement for their study course.

Essays should be required at every meeting, and they should bear upon the chapters of the book to be read at that meeting, being enlargements of some point made there, or discussions suggested by them. These essays—or, at any rate, some of them—should afterward be utilized in the regular society missionary meeting. Following the reading from the book, too, there should always be given opportunity for questions and discussions aroused by what has been read.

Current Events should be reported at each meeting

of the club. The best plan is to assign one member to a country and obtain reports from each in turn, this week from Burma, the next from South America, etc. Different persons should report for the home field in the same way, and at every meeting. A third report which might be given at each meeting is from one of the mission boards of your denomination, these being divided among the members, that they may keep track of their condition and work. Prayers for missions should also come in each meeting, as well as the reciting of memory missionary verses from the Bible. The work of each meeting should begin with a review of last week's work, and end with an examination on the day's work. The review should be oral, and the examination may often be written, although it should be very brief. At the close of each book or course of study a thorough examination should be given, one entire meeting being occupied with the review and the closing examination.

CHAPTER IX.

MISSIONARY LETTERS.

Helpful all Around. — Few bits of writing go through Uncle Sam's mail that do more good than letters to missionaries. They serve to make missions vivid to the writer as nothing else will. If written in a sincere, Christian spirit, they are of supreme value to the missionary, and hearten him for his work as perhaps nothing else can. A five-cent postage stamp affords us an easy and pleasant way of obeying to some extent the Master's command, "Go ye into all the world." It can carry a very real piece of ourselves to China, Madagascar, where we will. Let us have more consecrated postage-stamps.

The Use of Missionary Letters. — For this purpose societies should band together more than they do, and pass around good missionary letters, that the work of the missionary may go as far as possible. The missionary committees of the same denomination in a city or in neighboring small towns should co-operate to this end. I do not advise the manifolding of missionary letters. That, to me, takes all the personality out of them. It is better to pass them around ; and be sure to send with them the foreign envelope, with the stamp and post-mark! As these letters go to the various societies, how delightful it would be if in each society some member should be instructed to write to the missionary.

Be Thoughtful. — Missionaries are the busiest people in the world—more busy even than editors. There is no end to the things they may be doing, and they work under great pressure of responsibility and opportunity. Moreover, they are not chosen because of their ability to write, and though, of course, since they are persons of unusual intelligence, there is among them more than the average number of good and quick letter-writers, yet we must remember that to some of them, as to us, letter-writing may be a great task, and we must be careful how we require it of them. In entering into correspondence with a missionary, always express plainly your sense of these facts, and tell him that you will understand why no answer comes, if none does come, and be entirely satisfied. Moreover, assure him that any letter he may have time to send (and you may be sure that he will answer if he can) will be used fully for the arousing of new missionary zeal.

Be Regular. — What is not done systematically is likely not to be done at all. Set before you a definite aim in this letter-writing. Is one missionary letter a month from each Endeavorer too much to hope for? The letter may take half an hour to write (long letters are not needed). Is that too much time to give each month to this blessed personal work for the Master?

A Letter Evening. — When your plans are in full operation, you will wish to have an occasional letter evening, in the course of which *every member* of the society will read extracts from the most interesting missionary letter he has received during the last six months. Of course this will not mean that you have

obtained so many letters from the missionaries themselves; that would be too great a burden upon them.
Let a large part of your correspondence be with the
Christian Endeavorers. If you have not enough letters to fill out the entire evening, read what you have
and intersperse items about each missionary station
heard from.

Not Always to Missionaries. — It will aid the missionary work in many ways if, instead of always writing to the missionary, you get into correspondence
with the native Christians. Usually the missionaries
will have to write their letters for them at their dicta-
tion, but it will strengthen the faith of the natives,
help the missionaries get in touch with them, and
give you some of the most delightful letters you ever
read, besides giving you an opportunity to testify of
Christ to his new-found brethren over the seas. Especially, write to the native Christian Endeavorers.
What a stimulus it will be to their work, and to yours,
to emphasize in this way the sense of our world-wide
brotherhood! Every country now has its hundreds
of native societies, and each foreign land, of course,
has its strange Endeavor customs. Learn these
plans; they may well be worth transplanting. And
in exchange, tell them what your own society is
doing.

Christian Endeavor under Difficulties. — There are
places where Christian Endeavor especially needs
the help of your ink-stands. One of them is in prisons, and the rapidly increasing number of prison
Christian Endeavor societies should spur us to generous letter-writing for the benefit of our brothers in

bonds. The gracious custom has sprung up of writing them hearty personal letters at Christmas time and at Easter, and these letters do a world of good. Equally prized and equally helpful are letters to the Endeavorers on board ship, to the societies in asylums, and in other places where Christian Endeavor is maintained only with the exercise of a heroism many of us know little about.

The Home Fields. — It may seem more interesting to receive a letter from Yokohama than from Springfield, Mont. (if there is a Springfield in Montana); but if you are patriotic, you will not neglect the home field, and you will soon come to think quite as much of your home-mission letters as of the foreign. Indeed, as this correspondence can be conducted in the language familiar to both parties, it can be made much more interesting and valuable.

A Letter Committee. — In view of all these possibilities, do you wonder that I advocate the formation of a letter committee in every society? The work of letter-writing should be under the direction of the missionary committee, but they need much assistance, and the society needs to give it. The letter committee may be different each month, and should be chosen by the missionary committee, who will appoint one of its own members as chairman.

CHAPTER X.

MISSIONARY MUSEUMS.

Their Advantage. — As will be seen from the preceding chapters, missionary meetings need for their best success a large amount of illustrative material, and since our membership is changing and the work ever the same, it will greatly promote the missionary cause if the material gathered by one set of workers can be handed down to the next. It is human nature, when one has made a good map or obtained some interesting object from foreign lands, to wish to keep it, if only as a pleasant souvenir; but the spirit of the early disciples, who had all things in common, is the missionary spirit, and I am sure that missionary workers, as soon as the need is clearly shown them, will be glad to establish in a missionary museum a permanent fund of missionary helps.

The Room in which these objects are preserved should be the same from year to year, if possible. It is best some room in the church building or in the parsonage next door, but the museum may be set up in any private house.

Its Contents will comprise whatever may be of interest in the missionary meeting or suggestive to coming missionary committees. There will be curios, of course, from all lands, and especially foreign costumes. It will be hardest to get the members to part with these, but they will be most useful in carrying on the work. There will be articles of use or ornament from all around the world, idols, samples of food, commercial products. The flags of the various nations, for use in decorating, will be kept here, and will often be required. Missionary mottoes, diagrams that have been found effective, maps and charts of all kinds, will here be preserved. The essays that have been presented in missionary meetings will be placed on file here — or at least copies of them — together with the reports of all former missionary committees. Unless you wish to place the missionary library in the society meeting-room, here you will put your files of missionary magazines and your collection of missionary books and pamphlets.

Arrange the Museum carefully, placing in one compartment everything from one country. Provide a neat and complete catalogue of whatever you have. If duplicate copies of the catalogue can be prepared by a copying-machine, they will prove very useful.

Interest People in the Museum, especially the missionaries, and you will soon find treasures floating in upon you from all over the world. There is no reason, either, why you should not spend a little money upon it, since it is to be used to make money for the Lord, and a few dollars laid out in foreign costumes not easily obtainable otherwise might prove a fine investment.

Local Unions, of course, may do this work far better than individual societies, and wherever possible the missionary museum should be a union affair. It will then be placed in some central locality, and be given in charge of a union officer.   It may become a very large and important collection, and if care is exercised in appointing missionary meetings on different nights, or, if they are on the same night, in seeing that the subjects are different, there need never be confusion in the use of it.

CHAPTER XI.

MISSIONARY SOCIALS.

All Things to All Men. — The shrewd missionary worker at home will imitate the wise men that are at work on the missionary fields: he will not wait for men to come to him to learn about missions, but he will go to them; and he will not present his subject only in one stereotyped way, but in as many ways as he can think of. Especially, he will take advantage of the interest in play which all healthy young folks feel, and will carry on, now and then, a missionary social. The hard-worked social committee will be very glad to resign their post for the occasion, and allow the missionary committee to run a social as they please. The following brief accounts deal with types, and do not pretend to be exhaustive. For instance, the idea of a " Hindoo Social " may be applied to any missionary country, and so with most of the socials described. Thus these plans are susceptible of many applications.

A Foreign Games Social. — By correspondence with missionaries, by conversation with travellers, or from books, get a collection of the games of missionary countries, and devote an evening to playing them, interspersing the games with short missionary addresses. Here is a sample game from Japan: Place the Endeavorers in two long lines, facing each other.

The leaders step forward and say together, "One, two, three!" With the "three!" each thrusts forward simultaneously one hand, with the palm flat, or with the fist closed, or with only two fingers extended. If both have the same gesture, it is a tie, and the performance must be repeated; but if A has closed his fist, he has represented a stone; and if B has his palm extended, he has represented paper, and is victorious, as *paper can wrap up stone*. If, on the other hand, B had extended his fingers, representing scissors, A would have been victor, because *stone spoils scissors*. *Scissors cuts paper*, and so is victorious over it. The conquered player steps out of the line, while No. 2 in each row tries his fortune. So it goes on down the lines; then begins at the head again with those that are left, and continues until one side is wiped out.

A Curio Social.—Interest all the members of the society and their friends in gathering every possible article from foreign lands, especially those in which your church has missionaries at work. Arrange these on tables, or in prettily hung booths, in each of which there may preside a young woman dressed in the costume of the country, and ready to explain whatever is on her table. The Turkish room may have Turkish coffee to regale visitors; the India room may treat them to curry; the Chinese room, to tea or to lichee nuts, and so on. After all have passed around among the tables, call the assembly to order, and let some competent person give a lecture on the curios, telling about the strange customs they illustrate, and bringing in many a plea for missions by the way. Close with a missionary hymn.

A Cook's Tour. — To carry on a Cook's tour, and yet not leave town, first choose the country in which you will journey, — say, China. Next gather every possible article illustrating that country, and especially pictures of all sorts, photographs preferred. Hang these around the room, and place the objects — carvings, idols, pottery, vases, dresses, and the like — on tables. Divide these things uniformly over the room, and place in each section of the room a tourist conductor, who will know all about the objects and pictures in his section. Let the Endeavorers wander around as they wish until all are there. Then divide them into as many groups as you have tourist conductors, send each group to one section of the room, where the conductor will explain everything; then, at the tap of a bell, let the groups pass to the sections next in order, and so on, until the entire series of exhibits has been visited.

A Ceremony Social. — This form of entertainment is very amusing and instructive. It requires costumes and a pretty good knowledge of foreign customs, — but nowadays both can be obtained, if one has intelligence and knows how to use books. The ceremonies best suited to representation are a Turkish wedding, a Japanese ceremonial call, a Chinese tea, a Mohammedan salutation, worship before a Buddhist shrine, and the like.

A Missionary Quiz. — The scope of the missionary quiz must be announced several weeks beforehand, that the members may study up. It is best conducted by the pastor, who will manage it in the same way as the old-fashioned spelling bee, — only, instead of requiring the victims to spell our absurd English words, he will ask them questions in missionary history and other missionary facts. If the sides are chosen three or four weeks in advance, the leaders may be trusted to see that the members of their respective sides are well posted before the evening arrives. Confine the questions to one country or one missionary board. It might be well to give a good missionary book to the victor, but this should be a surprise.

Who Am I? — Each Endeavorer, as he enters, receives, pinned upon his back, the name of a missionary. He is to find out what missionary he represents by conversing with those he meets. They will talk with him as if he were the missionary whose name he bears, but of course without calling the name. He will do the same for them. When one has guessed who he is, the slip of paper is transferred to the front of his coat. This game will not go well unless the names of the missionaries to be used have been posted in some conspicuous place for several weeks beforehand, so that the Endeavorers may have a chance to study up. To vary the game, some may be given more general names to discover, such as a Hindoo widow, a Buddhist priest, the "Morning Star"; but this should be understood beforehand, or it will be confusing.

Mission Cities. — Divide the company into two groups, and place them on opposite sides of the room, with an umpire between. Allow each group a few minutes in which they may consult and make out a list of as many cities in mission fields as they can, beginning with A. When the umpire calls "Time," he will point to one side, whose leader promptly calls out the name of a city. Turning to the other side, the umpire counts twenty. Before he has finished, the leader of the other side must name another city. Thus it proceeds, until the list of one side is exhausted, when the other side is credited with that letter; and the two sides consult on the next letter. It will be in order for any member to whisper to the leader at any time the name of a city not on his list. If the umpire is in doubt whether the city is in a missionary country, he may compel the side that names it to tell where the city is. The side gaining most letters is the victor.

Missionary Clumps. — You are probably familiar with the game of clumps, in which the company is divided into two groups, which occupy different rooms, and send representatives — one from each clump — to consult together and fix on some object. The representative from each group goes before the other one, and is questioned until one group has found out what it is that has been fixed upon. A clapping of hands announces the victor to the defeated side. It will be of interest to play this on missionary lines, setting the Endeavorers to guessing such objects as Carey's hammer, Morrison's printing-press, Mackay's engine, Livingstone's heart.

Boston Translated. — The good old game of " Boston " may be given a useful missionary twist. Some one well informed regarding missions will preside over the game, and begin the story. This leader will assign to each player some name connected with the history of missions — either the name of a place or the name of a missionary. When in the course of the story any of these names is introduced, the person bearing it must at once rise and whirl around, on pen_ alty of paying a forfeit. When in the course of the story the leader comes to the word, "Calcutta!" all the players change seats, and in the confusion the leader also gets a seat. The person left standing must go on with the story, and so it continues until a sufficient number of forfeits has accumulated, when they must be redeemed.

A Tum-Tum Social.— Of course this social is not based exactly upon that Hindoo drum, but it is based upon the music of missionary lands. Make up the evening's entertainment, so far as possible, by the use of songs in the language of missionary countries. You will be able to get some natives to furnish it, per- haps,— some Armenians, Chinese, Japanese, Hindoos, Africans, or Indians. Solos on foreign instruments may be introduced. The songs of some of these countries may be obtained translated into English, but with the foreign music. Interspersed among these musical performances will come, of course, short talks about the various missionary lands and the work there.

Missionary Charades.— These are managed like the ordinary charades, except that famous missionary scenes are presented for the audience to guess— such scenes as Judson in his prison, or Gardiner and his comrades shipwrecked in Patagonia.

The Missionary Post-Office.— The missionary com- mittee will prepare a large number of letters, one for every member of the society. These letters will be written in the character of some foreigner, and will introduce as many foreign ideas and customs as possible. They will be also, in different ways, strong pleas for missionary work. Each envelope will bear the stamp of the country from which it is supposed to have come. Arrange part of the room in which the social is held as a post-office, and have each Endeavorer call for his mail. After each has received his letter, he must read it aloud. Introduce bits of fun into each letter, to keep up the interest.

Missionary Representatives. — A pleasant feature of some social not otherwise devoted to missions, would be the requirement that each person come wearing something to indicate a mission land. The entire costume or only part of it may suggest the country, and you may establish a contest, in the first part of the evening, to see which can make the most full and correct list of the different countries represented.

Hindoo Social. — The idea is to pack into one evening as much as possible about India. Hang the room with English flags and with Indian fabrics. Crowd it with all the articles from India you can get together. Have essays and talks on different phases of Hindoo life — the schools, the women, the farmers, the temples, the caste system, widows, and the like. Show on the wall as many pictures as you can gather. Hang up a map of India ready for reference. Have Hindoo songs, Hindoo ceremonies, recitations of Hindoo poems, quotations from the " Light of Asia," from some of Kipling's Hindoo ballads, summaries of the lives of the great missionaries to India. So much depends upon the resources of your town that no specific directions can be given ; but if you set to work and make a careful investigation, you will be astonished, I am sure, to see how much material you can bring together.

Quotation Envelopes. — A good feature for a missionary social is the bringing of envelopes in which each has placed some contribution for missions, while upon the outside is written a quotation from some missionary. After the contents of the envelopes has been counted and announced, the envelopes are distributed and the quotations read aloud.

Missionary Post. — This is for an outdoors social. Name the trees, bushes, etc., with the names of important stations in different fields. Large banners should be provided beforehand, each bearing the name of a station and also of a missionary at work there. The players posted at the several stations represent the missionaries there. One player, unassigned, stands in the centre. By motions the players arrange for exchanges of posts, Dr. Farnham of Shanghai, for instance, going to become Dr. Barnum of Harpoot. With each transfer, the player takes up a new character. While the change is being made, the leader tries to slip into the place temporarily vacant. If he succeeds, the outwitted player becomes leader in his turn.

Missionary Alphabet. — Give each player a piece of paper and a pencil. The game is to make — in five minutes, say — as long a list as possible of missionary stations and missionaries whose names begin with A. After this, pass to the following letters. The person victorious in the most letters wins the game.

Countries and Characters. — The leader stands in the centre of the circle with a knotted handkerchief which he throws at some player, at the same time saying, "A place in China," or, "A missionary in Turkey," calling for either a missionary station or a missionary in some country. If the person hit cannot answer before ten is counted slowly, he must take the leader's place in the centre.

Hidden Stations. — Divide the members into groups, and give to each person a slip of paper bearing say ten anagrams, each anagram being the name of some prominent missionary station, the letters all mixed up. The anagrams are numbered, and each group is furnished with a set of items, correspondingly numbered, concerning the hidden stations, no proper names being admitted. These are to serve as an aid for solving the anagrams. The first group to solve all the puzzles correctly (a member of the missionary committee with a correct list is stationed at each table) will announce this fact by clapping the hands, when the right list will be read aloud.

A Hunt for Facts. — Write upon slips of paper a number of missionary facts, making them as varied and suggestive as possible. Divide these slips, each of them, into two parts. As the members enter, give each of them one half of a fact, and tell them that on the stroke of a bell they are to hunt for the rest of their facts. It will add to the interest if half of each fact is given to a boy and half to a girl, so far as possible. After all have been matched, they should be read aloud.

An Examination. — If you have a very jovial person to conduct the examination, you can get a great deal of fun as well as profit out of such an exercise, held at the close of a missionary social at which essays have been read. The examination will be upon the information presented in these papers and during the evening. The questions should be few, and should call for only short answers. Pass the papers to your neighbors, correct them, and mark the per cent as the right answers are read. Honor in some way the person whose per cent is the highest.

A Missionary Hunt. — Tell the Endeavorers, before they come, to make themselves familiar with the various mission fields of their denomination and the names of the principal missionaries at each. As each Endeavorer comes in, give him a card bearing either the name of a missionary or the name of a station at which that missionary labors. On a given signal the stations set out to hunt for their missionaries, and the missionaries for their stations. Each pair must present themselves before the missionary committee to learn whether they are properly matched. If you want to make this social simpler, place in the room a home-made map on which you have marked the stations and the missionaries used during the evening. The Endeavorers can examine this, and learn for what name each is to search.

Sewing Bees. — If your church has no young women's missionary society, it probably has no sewing bees for missionary work with the needle; and what agency better to establish these delightful affairs than the missionary committee of the Christian Endeavor society? While the young women are sewing on missionary garments, let one of their number read aloud from some interesting missionary book.

An International Tea. — This may be made as elaborate as desired, with tables bearing viands of different countries, waiters dressed in national costumes, decorations of appropriate flags, the singing of national songs, and other fitting exercises. Put at each plate a card bearing information about the missions of the country represented by that table.

Missionary Nuggets. — This will furnish a pleasant half hour at any social. Distribute cards, upon which have been written famous bits from the writings of eminent missionaries. Upon the back of each is to be given a suggestive fact or two about the missionary, but no name. Each member in turn will read the quotation, and the information on the back of the card. Then the card is to be given to the person who first names the author. The Endeavorer that gets the most cards is the winner.

An Animated Missionary Library. — Each young woman is to represent a missionary book. She will post herself upon the contents of the book, and at the social will answer only questions with reference to it. The books will be given numbers, and the young men will "draw them" by number, without knowing who or what they are. Then the conversation is to begin, and is to continue until the young man has discovered with what book he is talking. Then he may draw another!

Picturesque Devices. — Be sure to select some bright feature in the life of each country presented in your socials, and hang upon it some missionary information. For example, if you are planning a Japanese social, you may buy a lot of little Japanese umbrellas (one cent each) and attach to each a set of facts about Japan—different facts for each umbrella. At a certain stage in the evening's proceedings, some one will read a set of questions to which these facts are answers, and as each question is read, whoever thinks he has the appropriate fact to answer it, will respond.

If your social is upon Alaska, set up in one corner of the room an Indian tepee, within which will sit a squaw, who hands to every one that calls on her a slip of paper bearing either a question or an answer upon Alaskan missions. The recipients are expected to hunt around and find the corresponding slip.

If you are dealing with China, construct a gay pagoda in one corner of the room, and hang upon it little pieces of red paper, each of them containing a missionary fact relating to China. These slips are of different lengths, and when all that have slips of the same length have come together, the assembly will be found to be divided into groups of fours. The information gathered by each four will be discovered to be on some one subject, such as Chinese education, Chinese religion, the Chinese language. It will next be in order for each group to read the slips of paper in their possession.

CHAPTER XII.

MISSIONARY MONEY.

The Aim.—It is not right to have much regard in our Christian Endeavor work to the total amount raised for missions. Most of our members are young people not yet earning money, and have little of it to give. The educational value of giving is what you must consider chiefly. It is essential, therefore, that every one give something, and that all gifts be made regularly. What you want is to cultivate the habit of giving. If the Christian Endeavor society does this, it is doing all that can fairly be expected of it.

The Envelope System.—This is the ideal way of raising money for missions; in fact, there is no other way worth consideration. At the beginning of the fiscal year the treasurer hands to each member of the society a printed card (it may be typewritten or hectographed, though you can obtain the cards already printed from the United Society). This card contains the statement that the Endeavorer will give during the coming year so much a month. There is a list of figures, from one cent to twenty-five or fifty cents, and the Endeavorer checks off the amount he thinks he can give each month. The treasurer then hands him a set of twelve little envelopes, each bearing the name of a month. He is given a number on the treasurer's book, and the envelopes are numbered to correspond.

There is nothing binding about the plan, but one may withdraw from it during the year, if he choose. I have yet to hear of a society that adopted this method, presenting the plan to each member personally, and ever afterward failed of a well filled treasury. It puts our gifts on a businesslike basis. Each knows what is expected, and the society knows what it will receive, and can plan accordingly.

Ice-Cream Zeal.— If in your church you are already well trained in the art of giving, it will not be so dangerous for you occasionally to raise missionary money by means of entertainments, suppers, fairs, and the like; but if your community has been in the habit of relying on such sources for most of its missionary gifts, the sooner and the more completely you break away from them, the better. "Pay socials do not pay." "Birthday parties" (a penny for every year of your age) are the death of true missionary giving. When we give ten cents for a plate of ice-cream in order that one cent of the dime may get to the heathen, our interest goes rather with the ice-cream than with the pitiful penny. That is not genuine giving which must go around by way of a strawberry patch.

When Shall We Receive the Missionary Gifts ?— At the monthly consecration meeting, of course. Then you are most sure of a full attendance. Besides, what you give to missions is proof of consecration, to that extent, at least, and fits into the very spirit of the service. Always follow the reception of the collection with a prayer that God may bless the gift, and that souls may be won through it.

How To Divide the Money Raised.— In some churches

less amply provided with this world's goods, the aid of the Endeavorers in maintaining the church may be very acceptable; but in most churches the young people will be free to use all their money for missions and to keep up their society work. In most societies the latter item is a very slight drain on the budget; the society expenses consist almost entirely of topic-cards, with a little now and then to eke out a social. Most of the Endeavorers' money, then, can be appropriated to missions, and it is best to divide it equally between the home and the foreign fields. Of course, if the society wishes, separate pledges can be made for missions and for the society expenses; but that seems a needless complication, if it is understood that most will go to the mission boards.

The Forward Look.— It is a decided advantage if the chief objects of your benevolence for the year can be selected beforehand, though of course you will wish to leave part of the probable receipts unappropriated to meet unexpected calls. But if you know what you are raising money for, it will be possible to arouse much more interest in the cause. Throughout the year you can not only speak of the good your past contributions are doing in certain fields, but you can urge the need of the fields to which you are intending to send money as soon as it may be raised.

A Programme of Giving.— An individual forward look at the beginning of the year, as well as one taken by the society as a whole, will be a good thing for missionary giving. Hand to each member a hectographed or typewritten copy of the following:—

It is my purpose to give each week during the coming year to each of the following objects the sum set opposite them:—

The church.
Missions.
The Sunday school.
The Christian Endeavor society.
The Christian Endeavor union.
Temperance work.
Religious periodicals and books.
Flowers for the church.

Of course the list will vary in different localities. Let the missionary committee place upon the board a copy of the list with sample figures added by way of suggestion, ranging from ten cents at the head to, possibly, one-fourth of a cent in the less important cases.

Separate Funds.— The older Christians find it a help to divide their missionary gifts, taking up separate collections for foreign work, home work, church-building, Sunday-school extension, and the like. It may well be that, as a mere matter of education, if for no other reason, it would be well in our Christian Endeavor societies to give an opportunity at least to each member to subscribe separately to the different missionary objects to which his society will contribute during the year.

How Should Money Be Sent to the Missionary Boards ?— Send it always through your church treasurer, because the Christian Endeavor society is a branch of the church, and whatever it gives should be counted in with the church gifts. However, the treasurer should be asked to keep a separate account of the Christian Endeavor gifts, and to designate them separately in sending them to the boards. This is because many boards wish to keep track of the amount of money sent by the Endeavor societies. If your money is to go to certain missions or missionaries set apart by the boards for the support of the young people, the treasurer will, of course, make that disposition of your gifts.

Follow Your Gifts.— You will have lost much of the value of giving, if after you have given you permit the society to lose sight of its gifts. Every dollar should mean just so much more of continued interest in some missionary field. For instance, you have sent fifteen dollars to a school in India: let the missionary committee see to it that subsequent missionary meetings present news from that special school, though they present nothing else. Read before the society whatever letter of acknowledgment comes to you. Get a letter from some missionary there, if you can. Show pictures of the building and the natives. Make the Endeavorers feel that they have actually made an investment out in India which they should follow with their interest and their prayers. So important is this work that it might well be placed in the hands of a special committee,— a committee of one, possibly,— which might be called the "following-up committee."

The Gifts of Church-Members.— Most of our Endeavorers are church-members, and their contributions to missions are made chiefly, as is right, to the church directly. It is only fair, however, that in reporting for Christian Endeavor statistics the gifts of Endeavorers, these sums should be included, and the treasurer should get from the church-members in the society a statement of what they gave through the church, as well as what they gave through the society. Of course this information should be kept private so far as names are concerned.

Your Own Missionary. — Most missionary boards have adopted the plan of assigning missionaries to single Christian Endeavor societies or churches, or groups of societies or churches, for them to support entirely. I earnestly advocate this scheme. Experience shows that when a society is thus embarked on some grand definite enterprise, its interest is not centred on the one field in which its representative is at work, but at once becomes deeper and broader than ever before. Do something heroic, Endeavorers! Get your board to assign to you a missionary of your very own. If you go at the task in the spirit of the pledge, you will be amazed to see how easily the money will be raised, and how blessed will be the spiritual results.

A Division That Increases. — In case you are not giving all your money to the support of one missionary, it is better to divide it among several foreign and several home mission fields, than to send it all to one. Each gift, though it may be a small one, will interest the society in the field to which it goes, so that a diversity of gifts generally means a widening interest.

A Finance Committee. — The great subject of giving may well absorb the energies of an entire committee, as well as of the treasurer. Most societies have too few committees, anyway. This committee, if you decide to form one, should not in any way interfere with the treasurer, but should confine its efforts solely to making the Endeavorers more generous. It will push the Tenth Legion, inform itself regarding the special needs of the boards and of the mission fields and report them, give items to the point in missionary meetings, and report from time to time what progress the society is making in the matter of giving.

Just How You Stand.—Frequent reports from the treasurer will serve to maintain the society's interest in giving. At every business meeting he should tell precisely how the money is coming in, what has been spent, and for what missionary objects, and how much is left in the treasury.

A Record that Takes Care of Itself.—The treasurer will be saved some bother if he places a mission box in one corner of the room, and above it a list of the members of the society, each name being followed by fifty-two spaces, if the contributions are to be made weekly, or by twelve spaces if they are to be made monthly. Then, as the member places his gift in the box, he will place a cross opposite his name. The treasurer alone knows for what pledged amount each cross stands. He will take out the money every week at the end of the meeting, and count it.

The Tenth Legion.—Few branches of Christian Endeavor work have shown more clearly the practical common sense of the movement, together with its lofty ideals, than the Tenth Legion. This is an enrolment of tithe-givers, Christian Endeavorers and others. Its members simply state that it is their practice to give to the Lord's work one-tenth or more of their income. They receive a certificate, which is returned if, for any reason, at any time, they wish to give up this plan of giving. But only two or three of the many thousands that have enrolled have discarded the method. Indeed, a large number of them have gone on to give one-fifth or more!

There is nothing formal about the matter. It is anything but a return to Judaism. The movement simply springs from the knowledge that Christians in general are giving far less than one-tenth, and from the conviction that "gospel liberty" does not mean liberty to be less generous than the Jews.

To push this movement, send to the United Society of Christian Endeavor, and they will send you, free, a leaflet giving full details of the movement, with blank application-cards. They sell for two cents an address by myself which is to be illustrated by easily made paste-board designs, setting forth how little is now given and how much is needed. It is called, "The Tenth Legion." This may be repeated at a meeting called to arouse interest in tithe-giving. The United Society also sells — at fifteen cents a hundred — voting slips to be used to ascertain what part of your society are already tithe-givers, what part would like to be, what part keep regular account of their gifts, etc. The address referred to, another address by your pastor, short testimonies from those that have already tried the system of tithe-giving, and the voting (no names being given) — this would make an effective presentation of the case, and would constitute one of the most useful of missionary meetings. Try it.

A Standing Hint. — We do not use half enough in our religious work the principle of advertising. Try it in the matter of giving. Keep standing before the society, printed on a blackboard or on a sheet of card-board, this pointed announcement: —

Eight of our members
are now giving
the tenth.

SHOULD NOT YOU?

Of course the first figure should be changed as the number grows.

" My Account with the Lord." — Get some printer to print this title upon a set of little blank books, and give one of them to every Endeavorer, obtaining a promise to keep account in that book on one side of all receipts, and on the other side of whatever gifts are made to the Lord's work. Even if the system of tithing is not in every case at once adopted, yet the gain in generosity that will result from this regular keeping of accounts will pay for the books many times over.

Two Cents a Week. — The plan does not compare in value with the tithing system already mentioned, but some societies may wish to adopt, as a stepping-stone to a more just proportion, the "two-cents-a-week plan." In accordance with this, each member promises to give at least two cents a week for missions, paying the money every month to the treasurer, who keeps individual accounts. This may be increased to two cents a week for home and two cents for foreign missions, and then you may advance to the more liberal plan of the tenth.

A Growing Wave. — Some societies have found it profitable, in managing the "two-cents-a-week" plan of giving to missions, to ask each person that promised two cents a week to make a further promise that he

will endeavor to get two other persons to give in the
same way. Such a scheme might work, also, in the
propaganda of the Tenth Legion.

A Day's Wages. — If you find it hard to persuade
the young folks to give a tithe, approach those that
are earning salaries with the request that each of
them set apart at least one day's wages for the mission cause. This will doubtless be more than the
average gift to missions, and will mark a step in
advance.

Free-Will Offering. — These are commanded, in addition to the regular gifts that we pledge. Give an
opportunity for them by establishing a thank-offering
box in some part of the society room, whose contents
the treasurer will investigate every week, and report
frequently to the society for the sake of stimulating
such extra gifts.

A Birthday League. — This is a "wheel within a
wheel." It is made up of those Endeavorers that
agree to give each year on their birthdays a certain
sum to the missionary treasuries. The sum is supposed to grow larger as they grow older. Christians
outside the society are added to the league, and in one
instance known to the writer very large sums indeed
have been obtained in this way.

A Sacrifice Social. — Let the members agree to see
for a certain time — say a month — how much money
each can save by little acts of self-denial. At the
"sacrifice social" let each tell — in prose or verse —
how much he saved, and what he did without in order
to make the saving. Some societies have emphasized
this plan by giving to each member a "self-denial

box " or a self-denial envelope," to keep in plain view as a reminder.

An Object Lesson.—A meeting with this title may be made to teach a great deal about giving. Give each Endeavorer some figures and ask him to illustrate them in some way before the society at the next meeting. Help those that are not inventive. For example, what the nation pays each year for confectionery may be illustrated by an immense stick colored to represent a stick of candy, and our gifts to foreign missions by a pasteboard Bible made correspondingly small. The relative gifts of the different denominations may be represented by pieces of ribbon of different lengths. Diagrams may be drawn representing the average number of heathen to one missionary, and the average number of church-members to one minister at home.

Printers' Ink.—Invest in some good book on giving, such as Pansy's capital "Pocket Measure," or get from "Layman," 310 Ashland Ave., Chicago, a supply of his admirable "What We Owe, and Why We Owe It," which he will send you free. Then see that every one in the society reads these noble sermons on generosity.

Bible Spurs.—A meeting with this title may be based on Bible texts on giving. Hand one of these to each member, and ask him to read it at the meeting and follow it up with remarks of his own. Songs about giving, prayers for the spirit of self-denial, and an address on generosity will round out the meeting.

One Board a Meeting.—Until the members of the society are thoroughly informed regarding their mis-

sionary boards, it will be well for the missionary
committee to obtain ten minutes at each meeting (five,
if no more can be got) for the presentation of interesting items concerning the work of some one board.
Begin with an account of the work in general, and
then, after this survey has been made, go on to give
more details.

Shares in Missionaries. — It will give a delightful
sense of participation in missionary work if the members are invited to take shares in live missionaries or
native workers. Find what it costs to support some
particular missionary, divide it by one hundred or
one thousand, and ask each Endeavorer how many
shares he will take in the work of that missionary.
If you can undertake the support of a missionary
alone,—and many societies could do even this and
some are doing it,—get your board to assign one to
you, and then divide his salary into 365 parts, asking
each member for how many days he will have the
work of that missionary all to himself !

CHAPTER XIII.

RELIEF WORK.

Why Undertake It ?—There is always danger in theory without practice, and one of the chief advantages of the Christian Endeavor Society is that it always combines the two. We must manage to get personal missionary work into our missionary activities, or the missionary studies and even the missionary giving will fail of their highest service. It is for this reason that work in the prisons and in the hospital is so valuable, and it is for this reason that I urge young people, even though the means at their disposal may be slight, to take a hand in the relief work that all Christian churches should be carrying on. There are other reasons, also, why this relief work is fitted to our societies. Young people can learn the needs of the poor more readily than their elders without seeming obtrusive, and gifts will be received from them by the proud far more readily than from grown men and women.

Go With Your Gift.—Of course much of its value, to you and to the recipient, depends upon this. The missionary committee should not do all the work of distributing alone. Each special case of want should be placed in the hands of some one member who will become acquainted thoroughly with the person or family, so that whatever is given will come from a personal friend rather than from a stranger.

Learn Who Are in Need from your own observation, in the first place. Use your eyes in your own neighborhood, or, if you are in the city, take districts and explore them. If charitable organizations exist already, put yourselves under their guidance. Get from the doctors and from your pastor the names of the very poor and their addresses. You will not need to search long.

What To Give. — Clothes to the children, especially. Urge your desire that they may be able to come to Sunday school, and you will more easily prevail upon the parents to accept your aid. Gather cast-off clothing from the entire congregation. Do not forget toys. Many a nursery would be a more joyful place if part of its toys went to the children that never have such things. Give food, or money to buy it. Give coal where the fuel supply, that prime source of comfort, has run short. Give a doctor's care to the sick, or money to buy medicine. Indeed, the needs will be so numerous that you will not find it necessary to inquire what to give, but rather how to get the many articles urgently called for.

The Best Help Is Self-Help. — Whenever possible, give them work to do. It may be household sewing or family washing, or the garden to tend, or the lawn, or the front walk. It may be a situation in a store. The very best relief committee is an employment bureau.

Money for This Work must come largely from your elders, but lack of giving usually means only lack of knowledge, and if you will learn about such sad cases as are to be found everywhere, you will not need to do more than state them to open pocketbooks as wide as you please.

The Country Week or the day's outing is a matter for the unions, but if you have no local union, there is no reason why a single society may not do splendid work, although limited, in this very direction. Certainly those of you that have carriages can make missionary carriages of them, and see that they are often used to give rides to the children, the sick, and the weary, of the very poor.

A Rummage Sale has been found by some societies to be a good plan. It may be held in the church, or, if that is not in the neighborhood where many poor people live, it may be brought closer to them. It will consist of all the partly worn articles you can gather from the homes of the congregation, neatly set forth and classified on tables, and offered for sale at nominal rates. There will be a one-cent table, a two-cent table, and so on. The greatest care must be exercised to avoid giving the affair a patronizing tone, but that is true of all relief work. It is easily spoiled, but the spirit of Christ can fill it with all loveliness.

CHAPTER XIV.

MISSIONS IN THE JUNIOR SOCIETY.

A Very Full Treatment of this subject is given in my Junior Manual, and I must refer my readers to that book if they wish a large number of working methods. I can give in this place only a few general suggestions and a few specimen ways of working, especially some plans that are not described in the volume referred to. Indeed, most of the different kinds of meetings of which I give an account in the present manual may be made suitable, with little change, for the Junior society.

Children's Mission Bands are not found in some churches, but all the work of such bands is carried on, to save multiplying organizations, by the Junior society. When this is the case, the Junior superintendent must use double care that the missionary cause may not suffer but may rather be the gainer because this trust is committed to Christian Endeavor hands. Get into close touch with the denominational organization that conducts the mission bands; it is usually the woman's board. Learn the plans of the secretaries, use their leaflets and exercises, and let them know that your Junior society is co-operating with them as thoroughly as the best mission band in the country.

A Flag Exercise may readily be constructed, if you have a supply of foreign flags. Give each Junior some missionary fact or anecdote and have him step forward and tell it, at the same time waving the flag of the country about which he is speaking.

A Question Meeting may be made so simple that all the Juniors can take part. Ask each Junior a question about missions so very easy that he can get the answer almost anywhere; such questions as: "What are the mission boards of our church?" "Who was the first English missionary to India?" "What mission field is called the Dark Continent, and why?" "What mission field is called the Neglected Continent, and why?"

The Chairs may be made an interesting and ever-varying factor in a Junior missionary meeting. Place them in squares for cities, each city bearing a banner with its name upon it. Of course the Juniors that sit in these chairs are the people living in those cities, and will describe their surroundings. So the chairs may be made to represent islands, and a Junior may represent a missionary ship cruising among them. So in many other ways the children's vivid imaginations may be enlisted in the cause.

A Paton Sunday. — This will be a meeting entirely devoted to learning about the interesting life of this missionary, and it may be followed by other biographical meetings. In the same way you may have a Foochow Sunday, studying that interesting city and its missions, followed by a Calcutta Sunday, and the like.

Missionary Essays, brief and simple, may be given at every meeting. They will use up only a few minutes. On one Sunday an Endeavorer from the older society may give one and on the next Sunday a Junior, and so they may alternate.

Missionary Cardboard. — Cut out sets of cards, two by four inches, using a different color for each missionary country. Upon these cards write interesting missionary facts and anecdotes, or cut from the papers and paste them on, not by any means forgetting pictures. These cards may be used in missionary meetings, and should be kept as souvenirs by the Juniors participating.

"The Junior Missionary." — This would make a good name for a little manuscript missionary paper, to be edited by one of the Juniors, and read at every missionary meeting. Of course contributions are to be obtained from as many of the Juniors as possible.

Mission Maps made in the sand may teach the Juniors much about the mission fields. Dampen the sand beforehand, and use blue cambric on the bottom of the tray to represent the water. Dress dolls in foreign costumes for the people. Have the boys make paper models of foreign houses, of temples, pagodas, and the like. Get each Junior to make something for the map — a mission school house, a mission church, a mission college; and as each places his contribution in the proper position, he is to tell the society something about it.

The Birthdays of Missionaries may be observed by the Juniors, and if they send to the missionaries, in time to reach them on their birthdays, some little token of their love for them, it will cheer the missionaries beyond measure, and at the same time quicken the Juniors' interest in the work.

Souvenirs of Missionary Meetings will please the Juniors. They may be very simple, but they should be appropriate and should be given to each member present. For example, a good souvenir of a meeting devoted to studying missions among the Indians would be an arrow cut from pasteboard, gilded, with a blue ribbon tied to the shaft, and with the date printed on the back.

Foreign Christian Endeavor Badges may be obtained from the United Society, and may be used in various ways, as rewards and otherwise, to stimulate interest in missions. The Juniors will be proud to wear Chinese pins, and the little silver tokens will often remind them of their almond-eyed brothers and sisters.

Missionary Links. — These are obtained by correspondence with the Juniors of other lands. They consist of brief messages, especially Bible verses, written on uniform strips of paper sent for that purpose, though a fine effect is sometimes produced by the substitution of foreign paper. The messages should be written in the foreign languages, with translations following. They will be fastened together in a chain, and will hang in the Junior meeting-place as a perpetual reminder of missions and of the Juniors' kinship all around the world.

Text-Chains may be made for the sick in the hospitals or in the homes of the congregation. Each Junior chooses a Bible verse that he thinks likely to comfort and help the sick one. The text is then written, as nicely as he can do it, on a strip of bright-colored paper furnished by the superintendent, and when all are done, they are pasted together in interlacing links and sent to cheer the hospitals and the sick rooms. The children themselves may do much good by visiting the hospitals, old ladies' homes, and the like, singing to the inmates, and bringing them fruit and other delicacies, as well as light scrap-books they have made themselves and fans covered with funny stories or pretty pictures.

Talents. — Give to each Junior a small sum of money, say five cents, to increase for the missionary contribution. The children will buy with it material which they can make up into objects for sale, which can again be converted into new material, thus con-stantly adding to the fund. A social should be held, or some special meeting, to which the Juniors will bring their money and tell how they gained it.

Mite-Boxes will be of assistance in teaching the Jun-iors to save money for missions. They can be obtained at most missionary headquarters. Once a year, or oftener, hold " inspection " socials, in which the mite-boxes are opened and their contents counted.

Junior Gardens. — Set the Juniors to raising money for missions by means of gardening. Give each of them at the beginning of the season, in a bag, a cer-tain number of beans to plant, say one hundred and fifty, and at the close of the season have a " bean sup-per," all the articles of refreshment beginning with B. The beans from each garden are to be weighed and bought at their market value by some missionary grocer.

Missionary Canvassers. — The Juniors will make good canvassing agents for the papers published by your denomination, and since in most cases a liberal pre mium is allowed, this is one excellent way to raise money for missions. Another good way is to present each Junior with a prettily made Junior shield,— pasteboard, of course,—bearing upon its back ten little envelopes in two rows. Each envelope is to receive ten cents for missions, so that the whole when filled will mean one dollar.

A Parasol Social. — Provide little Japanese parasols, which cost about one cent apiece. Give one to each Junior. Attached to each parasol is a card bearing a missionary fact. Corresponding to these facts is a set of questions which will be read later in the evening, each Junior watching to see when a question is read that may belong to the answer on his parasol. For instance, if the question is read: " What do the Japanese street Arabs say to the foreigners? " The answer would be, " His talk is all the same as a cat's." " How many Chinese can read? " " How many missionaries are there in the world? "—that is the kind of question to propound.

Missionary Anagrams. — This is a pleasant missionary game for a social. Group the Juniors in companies of ten, and give each Junior a slip of paper with numbers from 1 to 10. Pass around in each group a set of ten cards, each card bearing the name of a missionary well known to the Juniors, but the letters all mixed up. They are to solve the puzzles, writing the names of the missionaries opposite the proper figure, each card bearing a number. Those that solve the greatest number in a certain time win the game.

CHAPTER XV.

UNION MISSIONARY WORK.

Other Chapters of this book have described fully some of the most important missionary enterprises of Christian Endeavor unions, namely, the missionary conference, the missionary mass meeting, the missionary museum, and missions in conventions. This chapter is to speak of other lines of work that do not need detailed treatment.

The Union Missionary Committee consists of the chairmen of all the missionary committees in the union. This committee itself has a chairman chosen by the union. The committee should meet several times a year to plan the committee conferences, and to arrange for whatever practical missionary work the union may carry on.

An Advisory Board. — Many lines of effort, noble in themselves, are not appropriate for an interdenominational body such as the Christian Endeavor union. Still other kinds of work, though suitable, require for success the advice and guidance of older heads. Every Christian Endeavor union should have, therefore, a pastors' advisory board, consisting of representative pastors of the different denominations, and new undertakings of importance should first receive the hearty approval of this board. Some of the plans suggested in the following pages would be very unwise under certain circumstances which the pastors alone could determine, though all such plans are described here for the reason that in some cities they have proved great successes, and have met with the cordial approval of all the pastors.

Your Own Mission. — Such a plan, for instance, is the adoption of a city mission, or the support of a city missionary. In some localities this has been the life of the city union, and has done wonders for the spiritual condition of the churches connected with it. Whether this is feasible or not,—and it generally is,— you may always give great aid to the city mission or missions by regular systematic assistance in their meetings. On one night, by previous arrangement, the Endeavorers of the Walnut Avenue Baptist Church will go to the Third Street Rescue Mission. The next night the young people of the Sixth Presbyterian Church will go there, and so on. These Endeavorers will help by singing, by their sympathetic, eager listening, by their cordial words to the men, by their ready, pointed, brief testimonies when called on, and by their faithful prayers. Of course the sights they will see and the words they will hear and this experience in actual evangelistic work will do far more for the Endeavorers than they will do for the mission ; but that is all the better.

Mission Sunday Schools are well within the scope of most Christian Endeavor unions. Established by the aid of the whole union, each school might be carried on by the Endeavorers of a single denomination, all the societies of that denomination uniting, so that there will be no trouble about the denominational affiliation of the church that will surely in time spring from the school. Officers and teachers will be drawn from the young people, and the hand-to-hand work with the neglected families of the city that will result from contact with their children will prove of inestimable value, not only to the city but to the Endeavorers as well.

Union Study Classes for gaining missionary information have been carried on in several large cities. The large numbers thus brought together furnish an element of enthusiasm wanting in smaller classes, and the friction of mind on mind is worth much. Besides, banding together in this way, the Endeavorers are enabled to obtain the finest of instructors. One union that tried this plan added to it a normal class for missionary leaders.

A Circulating Library of missionary books has been established by at least one union and found to be a success. The union buys the books at a discount. They are sent through the mail at a slight cost, and thus the reading of the very best missionary books is made possible for all the missionary workers of the union.

An Evangelistic Campaign waged by the young people alone has been carried on with much profit in some cities. Of course the pastors gave cordial assent — that is true of all these accounts. Committees were appointed — executive, devotional, evangelistic, finance, ushers, music, press, canvassing. The best of speakers were obtained, but the young people did most of the speaking themselves, after the Christian Endeavor fashion. Meetings were held night after night in the separate churches, and many were brought to Christ.

The Gospel Wagon is a missionary tool that young people will find very effective. Indeed, it has already been used to the greatest advantage by groups of Christian Endeavor societies. The wagon itself, with a Bible-rest for the speaker, with a portable organ, and with seats for a goodly company of singers, can be bought for a sum within the reach of most unions. By its aid the distant parts of the city can be reached, and the outlying districts.

Outdoor Evangelistic Services, with or without the aid of the gospel wagon, though they fall rather heavily on a single society, yet when all the societies in the union join together, they can be maintained without trouble. Most of the Endeavorers will sing, but many of them will testify, and their warm words for the Master will often produce an impression that the most eloquent preacher could hardly make.

In Factories. — From outdoor work to evangelistic work indoors is a short step, and the union will soon take it. The Endeavorers, wherever they have tried it, have been remarkably successful in reaching with the gospel companies of workers in the mills, the factories, the great stores, the street-car employees, men at the life-saving stations, men on the wharves, men in the engine houses, railroad men, the "shut-ins" of the asylums, hospitals, almshouses, and prisons. Just a simple Christian Endeavor prayer meeting, with hearty singing and plain, prompt, glad testimonies, such as Endeavorers are perfectly familiar with, has proved to be the best possible way into the hearts of many of these people whom the church too often neglects.

Bicycle Evangelists. — It has been found possible in some localities to gather a strong company of Christian Endeavor bicyclists, who — on week-day nights — set off on their wheels for the country districts in need of gospel work, and hold meetings in school houses and in similar places. What kind of "club outing" is equal to that?

There Are Many Other Plans which the Christian Endeavor union might carry out for the benefit of the mission cause. It might own and lend a magic lantern. Flower missions are carried on by many city unions, in conjunction with country unions. Fresh-air work and country week; street-car rides for the children of the poor; boat excursions, also, for them; carriage rides for their sick; regular meetings in country school houses — these are only a few of the diversified missionary undertakings that our active unions have proved possible for young people.

The State Unions have, as yet, developed few plans for advance missionary work, though some of the State unions have their missionary superintendents. Of course one of their first duties is to urge in all societies the appointment of missionary committees and the holding of regular missionary meetings, the circulation of missionary literature, and the formation of missionary study classes. Care for the missionary features of the annual Christian Endeavor convention also comes within the province of the missionary superintendent.

The First Work of a county missionary superintendent, or a State superintendent, or the chairman of a union missionary committee, is to ascertain, if it is

not known already, just what the societies are already
doing for missions. Knowing this, he can go on to
make definite recommendations. A circular of in-
quiry, with blanks to be filled out, must be his first
official document. It must ask what is the annual
gift of the society to missions ; how often they hold
missionary meetings ; what missionary themes are
taken up; what interest they have in special fields, if
any ; whether a missionary committee is in existence;
if so, the name of the chairman, and at what time the
new officers are chosen ; the name of the pastor, the
president, the corresponding secretary. Most of this
knowledge is necessary, and all of it is useful, before
wise work can be done in a union by those that would
stir up missionary zeal among its members.

State Missionary Campaigns, and even campaigns
that have extended through several States, have been
carried on with much enthusiasm and lasting gain by
the Endeavorers. The State officers manage the
work. They correspond with the societies, and, making the condition that the pastors shall first approve
everything, they arrange for such mass meetings as
are described in the chapter on that subject. The
local union agrees to pay its share of the speakers' expenses. An average of five dollars a union has been
found to be sufficient, as the speakers give their time
and only travelling expenses are to be provided for.
The best missionary orators in the country can be obtained for these campaigns, because the audiences offered are so large and so numerous. Night after
night, for several weeks at a time, the speakers move
from town to town, finding everywhere that the En-

deavorers have thoroughly advertised their meetings, and that a great throng of interested auditors awaits them.

Summer Schools of missions have been established for some time in at least one State, — California, — and they have done much good. The best of instructors are obtained, and the pleasures of a delightful vacation resort are combined with the greater joys of missionary study classes and lectures. As all States now have Student Volunteers, this plan, on a small and modified scale possibly, is one that may be transplanted from California.

CHAPTER XVI.

MISSIONARY MASS MEETINGS.

The Value of Numbers. — The phrase, "poorly attended," has come almost to belong to the words, "missionary meeting." I am thankful to say that in our Christian Endeavor societies the missionary meeting is usually the most popular of all the meetings. This will be true everywhere throughout the church if popular methods are used. It is only necessary to put together half a dozen "poorly attended" missionary meetings, and you have a crowded mass meeting that will excite the curiosity of the most listless and persuade the most indifferent that there must be something in missions worth his attention. Our churches have made the mistake of holding missionary meetings that treat only denominational topics, thus losing the impetus that should come with a great, world-wide movement like missions. In no town where it has been tried will there ever afterward be a doubt as to the value of the interdenominational missionary mass meeting.

The Speaker may be a returned missionary. If he is a good talker, of course he is the very best man for your purpose. He will welcome the opportunity of addressing a large audience, and will have much to say that is just as helpful to other denominations as to his own. Of course no collection will be taken, but

the meeting will have its effect on all subsequent missionary collections.   If no returned missionary is
available, nevertheless you may have a missionary
mass meeting, using some eloquent pastor or layman ;
or, perhaps better, use some of the following plans
which call for many speakers.

A Pastors' Meeting. — In this meeting every pastor
in town is to have a part.   Get a bright presiding officer who knows how to keep the speakers strictly on
time, while keeping them and every one else in a good
humor.   Divide the time evenly among the speakers.
Get each man to choose some aspect of missions on
which he would like to speak.   See that the titles are
taking ones, and advertise them all.   Never mind if
two do choose the same theme.   Each will have so
short a time that they will not be likely to overlap.
And with such a galaxy of able speakers, you will
surely have a crowded audience and a fine meeting.

A Testimony Meeting. — "Why I believe in missions" is the theme.   Choose for the speakers some
bright business men, a few attractive women speakers,
a teacher, a lawyer, a physician, and the like, covering
as wide a circle of occupations as you can.   Get the
best speaker in the community to sum up the argument in a few pointed sentences at the close.

A Bird's-Eye View Meeting. — Obtain for this meeting as many representatives of different denominations
as you can, and let each come prepared to speak on
the most important features of the missionary enterprises of his church.   Urge every speaker to stick
strictly to his text — not to make a plea for missions
in general, but to confine himself to telling in what

points his denominational missions are unique, and what conspicuous triumphs they have won or are winning. A large map would be of much service in this meeting.

A Generosity Meeting. — A number of speakers will make a plea from different standpoints for more generous missionary giving. One will make the argument from the Bible, one from the needs of the heathen, one from the commercial advantages that spring from missions, one from the heroic lives' of missionaries, one from the spiritual results among the heathen, and so on. Be definite. Push tithe-giving. Let the system be strenuously presented by some strong advocate who will invite questions about it from any one in the room.

A Missionary Jubilee. — This meeting might be held at the end of the year. Representatives of the different denominations would speak, each telling of the missionary victories during the year on the mission fields of his own denomination. The meeting would send every one home tingling with fresh zeal and new courage.

A City-Missions Meeting. — If your union is in a large city, you can easily obtain addresses of thrilling interest from representatives of the various city missions — the rescue missions that work among men and those that deal with the women, the missions to the sailors, the all-night mission work, the industrial homes, the children's missions, the missions to the Chinese, Italians, Jews, and other nationalities. The meeting will arouse the Christians to labor for their own city as no recital from a single missionary, representing a single institution, could.

"For Our Country." — A home-mission meeting is especially suitable for a patriotic anniversary, such as the Fourth of July and Memorial Day. If you cannot obtain a genuine home missionary, get a number of speakers to make short speeches filled with anecdotes, each of them taking up one phase of home-mission work, such as work among the negroes of the South, among the mountain whites, among the Indians, Chinese, Mormons.

A Missionary-Committee Meeting. — This is to be an evening for the Christian Endeavor workers especially. The members of the missionary committees of the union will themselves fill up the programme with brief, telling speeches, a sort of sharp-shooting, Christion Endeavor fashion. A good subject for the evening might be, " Missions and the Young," with such subdivisions as these: " What Christian Endeavor is doing for missions." " Christian Endeavor in missionary lands." " The condition of children under heathen rule." " Young men who have made great missionaries." " Young women who have made great missionaries." " The young people in the native missionary schools."

A Question-Box Meeting would be as successful in a mass meeting as it is in the individual society, only, if you try it for a mass meeting, you must be certain to provide a sufficient supply of questions against the possibility that the audience may not choose to ask questions themselves. Get at least three well informed persons, who are good speakers and missionary enthusiasts, to answer the questions. Let one take one-third, and answer them. Then have music, and pass on to the next third. Then have a series of sentence prayers by the Endeavorers, another song, and the third set of queries.

An Education Meeting. — This meeting will deal with the importance of missionary information, and the delights of missionary reading. It will present some of the most fascinating missionary books, and will seek to start in many different centres some systematic plan of missionary study. Here is a possible programme: " Outline of a simple missionary biography." " Some fascinating bits from missionary lives." " Why read missionary periodicals? " " A broadside of specimen missionary facts." This broadside is a collection of the most interesting of missionary facts and anecdotes, given in swift succession by a dozen young people. " A plan for missionary study applicable to any church or society."

The Stereopticon is always a good medium for missionary information. Missionaries on furlough are coming more and more to use it in their addresses. If a union cannot find a missionary so provided, it may purchase or make a set of slides, and get a missionary to base upon them a delightful talk.

A Day's Programme. — Several marvellous campaigns for the arousing of missionary enthusiasm have been conducted by the Christian Endeavorers of a number of States, and the plan that works best is in its essentials this: The pastors all preach missionary sermons in the morning, referring to the coming meeting. In the afternoon there is held in a central place a conference of all the missionary workers in town, young and old. The various plans proposed in the chapter on missionary conferences may here be used. In the evening comes the mass meeting, in which all the churches unite.

CHAPTER XVII.

MISSIONARY CONFERENCES.

A Most Useful Method. — The missionary conference, though a local union method of work, is of such importance as to warrant a chapter by itself. These committee conferences illustrate one of the chief advantages of our interdenominational system. They focus upon each society the enthusiasm and practical discoveries of all societies in the city or town. The missionary conference is made up of all the missionary societies in the union, or, if the union is too large for that, then of all societies in a certain district of the city. In order to give the zest of difficulty, admission to the conference should be by ticket only, and each committeeman should be given a few tickets to hand to his friends who might like to be present. We must be training material for the missionary committees in the future.

The Best Time for the conference is in the fall, at the opening of a new season of work. If a second conference is held during the year, let it be in the spring, to gather up the methods that have proved most useful.

A Roll-Call of the societies may well stand at the opening of the conference. This will stimulate attendance, especially if the result is reported at the next union meeting. Do not have it a mere formal roll-call, but after the chairman of each committee has told how many members of his committee are present, have him give one plan for a missionary meeting on China, for instance, varying the subject of this symposium with each meeting.

The Programme of the conference is prepared by the union missionary committee, or, if you have no such committee, then by the union committee that has charge of the conferences in general. It should always contain two factors: papers or addresses carefully thought out beforehand, and informal discussions and conversations.

The Topics to be Treated are at least as numerous as the paragraphs of this book. Here are only a few of the most important themes which may be discussed, first in formal essays and then in brisk question and answer: "How to present missionary statistics in the most attractive way." "How to get the Endeavorers to read missionary books." "How to increase the circulation of missionary periodicals." "The best way of presenting missionary biographies in our meetings." "Utilizing letters from missionaries." "Do we give liberally enough? How can we increase the per cent of our giving?" "What is the best missionary meeting you have held in your society?" Let it be understood that every member of the conference is expected to come with something to say on every topic. Announce the subjects in the invitations to the conference. In appointing the speakers that are to lead off in the discussion, subdivide the topics as much as possible, so as to give as many as you can some definite work to do, and thus make sure of their attendance.

An Exhibit should be made at the missionary conference of all new matter for illustrating missionary meetings that may have been added to the missionary museum of the union, or, if you have no such institution, let each society bring whatever objects have contributed to the interest of its recent missionary meetings — any bright diagram or chart, or object from a missionary land. It would be a good plan to have read before the conference the best short paper presented anywhere at a recent missionary meeting, if you can get hold of it.

The Conversational Spirit must be gained for the conference, if you want it to be successful. Let the leader set the example by boldly interrupting any speaker or essayist with questions as they occur to him. A missionary question-box or answer-box will add to this feeling of informality. Make the missionary conference in reality what it is in theory, an earnest, friendly talk among the faithful servants of the King on the absorbing question of how they can best advance the King's business.

CHAPTER XVIII.

MISSIONS IN CONVENTIONS.

A Missionary Address of some kind should be part of practically every religious gathering of Christian Endeavorers. This is our one great theme, as it is the one great theme of the church of which the society is a constituent part. Assign the best speakers to this topic. Give them the best place on the programme. See that the wording of their subjects is bright and "fetching."

The Missionaries Themselves should be heard from, if any are present. Conventions that are favored with the attendance of many of these Christian heroes should set apart a special time for introducing them to the audience. Each will be received with rising and a salute, and then, if there is time, will speak briefly. "Why I became a missionary," would be an inspiring symposium in which not only the missionaries might take part but also whatever Student Volunteers are present.

A Model Missionary Meeting would form an attractive portion of the programme. Let it be given by the society in the convention's constituency that gets up the most wide-awake missionary meetings. A stereopticon lecture on missions, and a missionary exercise by the Juniors, may be obtained. An hour may be given up to a memorial meeting for the great missionaries of all denominations that have died during the year, the work of each to be reviewed by some one in especial sympathy with it. Many ideas described in the chapters on missionary meetings, mass meetings, and union missionary work, may be applied also to State conventions.

Open Parliaments on missions' will arouse missionary zeal as few other exercises, if they are led with force and discretion. The speaker should devote himself not to showing off, but to drawing out. He should propound question after question, such as: " What was your best missionary meeting? " " How do you increase the gifts of your members? " " Why do you believe in missions? " " What systematic studying for missions does your society do? " " How do you keep before the society the work of the boards? " He will call for votes : " How many of you belong to societies that have missionary committees? that have regular missionary meetings? four times a year? six times? eight times? How many of you have read ten missionary books? How many subscribe to a missionary magazine? How many of you believe in paying to the Lord's work at least a tenth of your income? How many of you belong to societies that contribute enough to their denominational boards for the support of a single missionary? " A special conference of missionary committees held later in the convention will carry on with greater fulness the discussions suggested by this open parliament.

Objections to Missions may be presented concisely by one speaker (who will be, of course, a strong friend of missions) and then answered by another speaker. The most effective way of giving this is in a dialogue, the first speaker bringing forward an objection which is immediately answered by the second.

A Missionary Table should be a feature of every convention, and if the convention is large, it may become a missionary room, where may be displayed a sample missionary museum, together with specimen numbers of all the denominational and general missionary papers and magazines. Subscriptions should be received for them. All kinds of devices for adding to the interest of missionary meetings should be shown.

Blanks May Be Circulated for the signature of the Endeavorers, that the advice of the speakers may become fixed in their purposes. One of these blanks should be an application for membership in the Tenth Legion. These blanks are to be obtained, free, from Secretary John Willis Baer, Tremont Temple, Boston. The other blank should be what has come to be known as a "policy blank." It is a printed form, varying according to the local needs, and is an agreement on the part of the Endeavorers to hold their societies as far as possible to a certain high standard of missionary work, such as six missionary meetings a year, a certain per cent of missionary giving, missionary study classes, missionary.libraries, and the like.

A Roll of Honor is a useful method of exciting interest in missions. Upon it are placed the names of all societies that have given during the year at least ten dollars to their denominational missionary work.

There will be many feet of this missionary roll, and as it is unrolled by an ardent speaker and draped around the room, a scene of enthusiasm is sure to follow.

CHAPTER XIX.

MISSIONARY SPURS.

This chapter is intended to contain a number of missionary methods, well worth describing, that seem to have no suitable place in any preceding chapter.

The Missionary Information Committee, like the ordinary "information committee" of any Christian Endeavor society, will report at the opening of every meeting. Its report will consist of brief, "catchy" items of recent missionary news. The report may be given by a single member of the committee, or by all the members, each of them contributing an item in swift succession.

The Use of Tracts is commended to our societies as a sure method of reaching many souls. Of course the tracts should be wisely chosen, should be absolutely free from cant, manly and sincere in their tone. Some Endeavorers put them to double use by printing the church notices on the back, then distributing them as invitations from house to house.

A Society Bookcase for holding the missionary library may be made to do double duty. It can be arranged with a desk on which the society secretary may write, and with compartments in which may be kept pledge cards, topic cards, and the records.

The Christian Endeavor Day Offerings should always be for the cause of denominational missions. No other cause is so appropriate to the day. Advertise the matter well beforehand. Urge the gift as a thank offering for the blessings of Christian Endeavor. Set apart the week before Christian Endeavor Day as a special week of self-denial, in order that the gifts may be worthy of the society and of the cause. Divide the sum received equally between your home and foreign missionary boards, and when the money is sent in, say that it is the Christian Endeavor Day offering of your society.

Essays on Missionary Subjects may be called for at the beginning of the year, the subjects to require some considerable study and the papers to be of some length and importance. Get the pastor or some prominent member of the church to offer a prize for the best essay, choose a representative committee to act as judges, and appoint an evening when all the essays may be read and a decision rendered.

Visits to City Missions may be made regularly by members of the society who will be sent out two by two for this purpose. Such visits, of course, will not take the place of visits by the society in a body, but will be more frequent. At the next meeting each pair of delegates will report what they have seen and heard. As all missions will be visited in turn, this will be quite an education in mission work, both for those that go and for those that stay.

A Missionary Week. — This will not be impossible if you have worked up well the missionary zeal of the young people. Gain the co-operation of all other missionary organizations in the church. Arrange for an exhibition of whatever missionary material you may have — curios, diagrams, and the like. In the evenings hold meetings, considering each evening some one phase of the multiform subject.

A Hectograph will be the missionary committee's right hand man. Home-made hectographs do good work, or, you can buy one at slight cost. The hectograph can be used for copying programmes, for advertising purposes, for making duplicate maps, charts, copies of missionary exercises, and for divers other purposes.

Missionary Note-Books may be bought and given to every Endeavorer with the request that they be carried in the pocket, and that a watch be kept for whatever fact and interesting anecdotes may be found relating to missions. They may also be used to record thoughts on missionary topics, Bible verses relating to missions, and many other matters useful in missionary meetings. They may serve also as account books for missionary gifts.

Missionary Circles. — This is an easy and effective mode of keeping up the interest in missions. Divide the society into groups, each with a chairman, and assign each group to some country. Expect a report from each group once every three weeks. These reports will contain only two or three brief items, so that several reports can be read in five minutes.

Papers for Missionaries. — In their isolated posts the missionaries find the weekly visits of a religious paper a comfort and assistance such as we can hardly imagine. No gift of the same cost is equal in real value for the missionary to the gift of a religious journal. All papers make special reductions in price when the subscription is for this purpose.

Gift Boxes. — Of course our societies know about missionary "barrels," and have packed, or helped to pack, many of them. Without this practical aid the missionary cause would now be far less advanced than it is. But how many have sent out missionary gift boxes? These are to contain not so much what is needed as what will be enjoyed — little articles of luxury such as a missionary cannot afford. Toys for the children will go into these boxes, "patterns" of pretty dresses, books of poems and stories, and — to express the idea in a single word — candy!

The Missionary Bible. — The missionary committee will do much toward training the society in the missionary spirit if they can persuade the members to commit to memory Bible verses bearing on missions. Select a number — say twelve — and give the list to all the members, with the request that the verses be committed to memory before the next missionary meeting. At that meeting ask all to rise that can recite them, and then choose some one to prove it!

Ask the Missionary Boards what work they have for you to do. Most missionary boards now recognize the young people's societies as valuable aids. Some have special secretaries for young people's work. Almost all of them get out leaflets of information intended for young people. If you write directly to headquarters, you will cheer them there and you will get the best of guidance.

The Week of Prayer was originally established as a world-wide concert of prayer for missions. It has not departed so far from its first purpose that it will not be appropriate for our missionary committees to make special effort to win the young people's interest in it. Get them to attend in a body and to add to the meeting the enthusiasm of a Christian Endeavor gathering, speaking promptly when opportunity is given for testimony or prayer.

A Win-One Band is a simple "wheel within a wheel," and the possibilities for good are so great that all missionary committees would do well to consider establishing one in their society. The band consists of those that agree, God helping them, to win one soul to Christ during the year.

THE LATEST ADDITION TO OUR MISSIONARY BOOKS

FIFTY MISSIONARY PROGRAMMES.

By BELLE M. BRAIN.

THE first portion of this very helpful book is devoted to suggestions for securing ideal missionary meetings. Another section is filled with helpful material for missionary programmes. By far the larger part of the book, however, is devoted to programmes for fifty missionary evenings, the programmes being entirely different. Nearly every mission field and all phases of the missionary subject are considered.

Full information for making interesting and helpful missionary meetings is given in connection with each programme.

Nicely bound in cloth; price, 35 cents, postpaid.

UNITED SOCIETY OF CHRISTIAN ENDEAVOR.

BOSTON AND CHICAGO.

FUEL FOR MISSIONARY FIRES.

By BELLE M. BRAIN.

"Where no wood is, there the fire goeth out."

This is a cloth-bound book packed full of practical plans for Missionary Committees. By following the suggested plans or programmes given in this book, your missionary meetings will be the brightest that you ever held. The best book of this nature ever published. Every thing tried and proved. Try it! Price, 35 cents.

"The book is bright, pithy, sententious throughout. The committee work is not done for you, but novel programmes and plans vivaciously tell you how to do it. There is a great variety. The book merits unstinted praise." — *The Standard.*

"The practical missionary worker, whatever her position and duties, may well exclaim, 'Eureka!' when she realizes what is in this little book. It contains not only so-called 'fuel,' but 'kindlings'; for its hints and suggestions are so fine and easily utilized that the least spark of missionary enthusiasm must serve to ignite them." — *Heathen Woman's Friend.*

"This little book should be in the hands of the missionary committee of every young people's society. It is just what is needed to guide them in conducting missionary meetings and ways of working." — *Canada (M. E.) Review.*

UNITED SOCIETY OF CHRISTIAN ENDEAVOR,

TREMONT TEMPLE, BOSTON.   155 LA SALLE ST., CHICAGO.

Student Missionary Campaign Library.

16 Volumes for $10.00.

This library contains sixteen of the most recent missionary books. They are all of acknowledged worth. The set cannot be broken. It is shipped from Chicago only, and at purchaser's expense. Price, only $10.00. The sixteen volumes are as follows:—

1. **Missionary Expansion Since the Reformation.** By Rev. J. A. Graham, M.A. Price, $1.25.

2. **A Mexican Ranch.** By Mrs. Janie Prichard Duggan. Price, $1.25.

3. **The Growth of the Kingdom of God.** By Rev. Sidney L. Gulick. Price, $1.50.

4. **Light in the East.** By Bishop Thoburn. Price, 85 cents.

5. **The Chinese Slave Girl.** A story of woman's life in China. By Rev. J. A. Davis. Price, 75 cents.

6. **The Official Report of the Third International Convention of the Student Volunteer Movement for Foreign Missions, Cleveland, 1898.** Price, 1.50.

7. **The Story of John G. Paton.** Told for young folks. Price, $1.50.

8. **Persian Life and Customs.** By Rev. Samuel G. Wilson, M.A. Price, $1.25.

9. **In the Tiger Jungle.** By Rev. Jacob Chamberlain, M.D. Price, $1.00.

10. **The Personal Life of David Livingstone.** By W. Garden Blaikie, D. D. Price, $1.50.

11. **The Life of John Kenneth Mackenzie.** By Mrs. Mary F. Bryson. Price, 1.50.

12. **James Gilmour, of Mongolia.** By Richard Lovett, M.A. Price, $1.75.

13. **Nemorama, The Nautchnee.** By Rev. Edwin MacMinn. Price, 90 cents.

14. **The Story of the Life of Mackay, of Uganda.** By his sister. Price, $1.50.

15. **Oowikapun.** By Egerton Ryerson Young. Price, $1.00.

16. **Hu Yong Mi.** Autobiography of Hü Yong Mi. Price, $1.00.

UNITED SOCIETY OF CHRISTIAN ENDEAVOR,
TREMONT TEMPLE, BOSTON.   155 LA SALLE ST., CHICAGO.

LEAFLETS FOR MISSIONARY COMMITTEES.

We publish a number of leaflets for Missionary Committees, among which are the following:—

A Live Missionary Committee. Its object, organization, and practical methods of work. By Frances B. Patterson. Price, three cents each; $2.00 per hundred.

The Missionary Committee at Work. By W. Henry Grant. Giving suggestions for meetings, subjects, and programmes. Price, three cents each; $2.00 per hundred.

Work for the Missionary Committee. By Rev. Francis E. Clark. Price, two cents each ; $1.00 per hundred.

Suggestions for the Missionary Committee. Neatly printed cards. Price, three cents each; set of five, ten cents.

A Missionary's Visit. A dialogue. By Mrs. J. L. Hill. Price, three cents each; $2.00 per hundred.

Christian Endeavor and Missions. By V. F. P. Price, three cents each; $1.50 per hundred.

Maps and Money. By V. F. P. Price, three cents each; $2.00 per hundred.

Money and the Kingdom. By Rev. Josiah Strong, D. D. This is Chapter 15 of " Our Country," and is of especial interest to all tithe-givers. Price, two cents each; $1.60 per hundred.

The Missionary Prayer Circle. Prepared by the Yale Missionary Band. Subjects for prayer in young people's societies and in private devotions, covering a period of twenty-six weeks. Price, five cents a dozen.

Missionary Reading Circle Slips. Pledges to be used in securing readers of missionary books. Twenty cents per hundred.

The Pocketbook-Opener. By Rev. J. F. Cowan, D. D. Interesting and profitable, as illustrating the different principles of giving. This is printed in imitation of an alligator leather pocketbook. Fifty cents per hundred.

Missionary Committee Report Blanks. The book contains a sufficient number of blank reports to last two years. Price, including postage, twenty-nine cents.

UNITED SOCIETY OF CHRISTIAN ENDEAVOR,

TREMONT TEMPLE BOSTON.   155 LA SALLE ST. CHICAGO.

EVENINGS WITH MISSIONS.

There is no excuse for a dull missionary meeting, if the missionary committee will use the material given in our several missionary booklets and exercises. Our series of "Evenings with Missions" covers the whole field of home and foreign missions.

Price, 10 cents each.

No. 1. Mexico. Justly called "the land of flowers," and our next-door neighbor; yet how little we know about it!

No. 2. The Indians. Two hundred and fifty thousand in the United States who have been driven from their old hunting-grounds. What are we doing for them?

No. 3. A Trip to Alaska. While the interest in Alaska gold is so intense, what more interesting subject for a missionary meeting than this?

No. 4. The Freed People. Freed in name, but imprisoned in ignorance. Learn what is being done for them.

No. 5. The Chinese in America. Is it right to sing —
"Peace on earth, good will" — if you please —
"To all nations and peoples" — except the Chinese?

No. 6. Immigration and Evangelization of the Great West. A very instructive and interesting exercise descriptive of the emigrant from his landing at Castle Garden to his settlement in the Great West.

No. 7. Romanism in America. Contrasting the Roman Catholic *restrictive* policy with the American spirit of independence and freedom.

No. 8. The Mormons. Do you really know much about this cancer which is at the very heart of our civilization?

No. 9. General Survey of the Home Field. A very instructive evening may be spent with this subject, showing the providence of God in the settlement of our country.

No. 10. India.
No. 11. Africa.
No. 12. China.
No. 13. Japan.
No. 14. Turkey.
No. 15. South America.
No. 16. The Island World.
No. 17. Arctic Missions.
No. 18. City Missions.
No. 19. Our New Island Possessions.
No. 20. Siam and Laos.
No. 21 Korea.
No. 22. Persia.

These subjects are always interesting. The leaflets give plenty of material for most excellent programmes. They describe the manners and customs of the people, the horrors of heathenism, and the splendid work of our devoted missionaries.

UNITED SOCIETY OF CHRISTIAN ENDEAVOR,
TREMONT TEMPLE, BOSTON.   153 LA SALLE ST., CHICAGO.

MISSIONARY EXERCISES.

These exercises are very complete, and are compiled especially to awaken interest in the foreign field. They contain the entire programme, including hymns and Scripture readings. A separate sheet comes with Numbers 3, 4, 5, and 6 for the exclusive use of leader and speakers.

No. 1. **A War Meeting.**
No. 2. **The Whole Wide World for Jesus.**
No. 3. **Lessons from the Lives of Great Missionaries.**
No. 4. **Saved to Serve.**
No. 5. **The Church and World-Wide Missions.**
No. 6. **The Ultimate Triumph of World-Wide Missions.**

Price, sample copy complete, 5 cents; twenty-five copies, 50 cents; fifty copies, 75 cents; one hundred copies, $1.50. Two copies of speaker's part free with each quantity order.

Portfolio of Missionary Programmes. By S. L. Mershon. This booklet contains twenty complete programmes for missionary meetings, together with suggested thoughts on how to have the most interesting meetings. Price, 10 cents.

MISSIONARY COMMITTEE HELPS.

We also publish a large number of helps for the Missionary Committee, including leaflets upon the work of the committee, report-blanks, collection-envelopes and boxes, maps, etc.

UNITED SOCIETY OF CHRISTIAN ENDEAVOR,
TREMONT TEMPLE, BOSTON. 155 LA SALLE ST., CHICAGO.

www.ingramcontent.com/pod-product-compliance
Lightning Source LLC
Chambersburg PA
CBHW021155020426
42331CB00003B/73